what's that growing in my sour cream?

?

BRAD GRABER

TO MY WONDERFUL
HUSBAND, JEFF.

*How you have managed to
put up with me all these
years is a miracle.*

FOR ME,
*it's been a dream
come true.*

dedication

tableof contents

More tableof **contents**

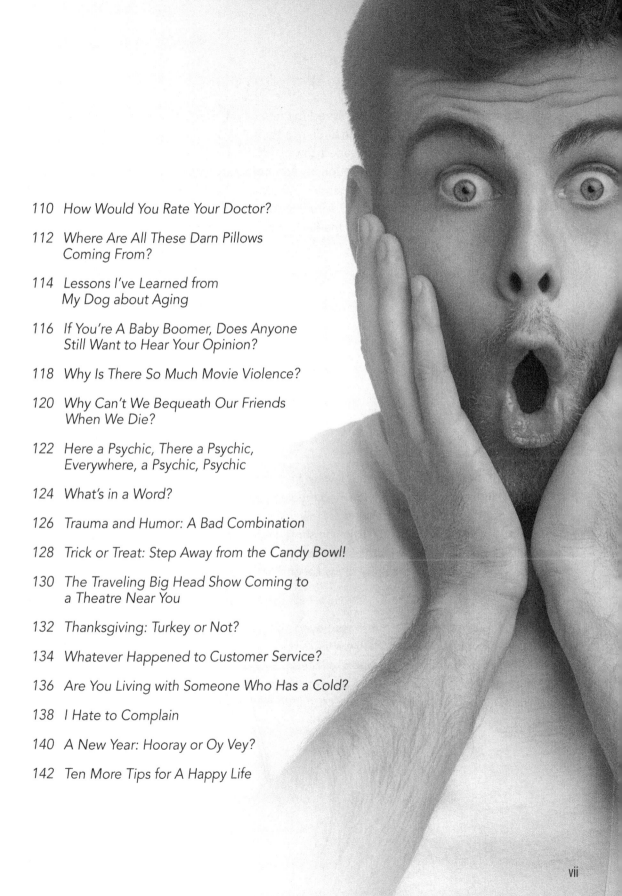

WHEN I FIRST STARTED WRITING A WEEKLY BLOG,

I was an unknown author. I'd just finished my first novel, *The Intersect*, and despite my best efforts was struggling to find an audience for it. In this new age of publishing, readers were "genre" driven. Tastes leaned toward Romance, Young Adult, Sci-Fi, Erotica, Mystery, Fantasy, or Paranormal. Though my contemporary fiction contained a minor love story, it didn't fit cleanly into a hot "genre." Should I add a dragon? Create an encounter with a UFO? Introduce wizards? Should my story have been set in the future when the Earth is inhabited by aliens living off the flesh of human livestock?

IN RETROSPECT, I SHOULD HAVE CONSIDERED IT.

But, that's simply not the fiction that I write. Perhaps one day, I'll give it a try. But for now, I'm all about how we connect and bring meaning to each other's lives. How friendships are formed. How families keep secrets. How injustice exists in plain sight and what good people do in the face of such injustice. In short, I'm fascinated with the human condition. Intrigued by the lessons we learn along the way. These are the themes that attract my attention. And if you pick up a copy of my second novel, *After the Fall*, you'll see that I still haven't learned the "genre" lesson.

But you shouldn't think that I'm a wild-eyed optimist. Not quite. I'm a realist at heart, with a radar for inconsistency. Perhaps that's because I was raised by a mother who often said, "Do as I say, not as I do." Upon reflection, and without any disrespect to Mom, that seemed pretty crazy. So, unwittingly, over the years, I've honed my skills at detecting inconsistency. And now, I'll let you in on a little secret: Inconsistency is everywhere. It's running rampant.

duction

WHICH BRINGS ME TO THE ESSAYS IN THIS BOOK.

You might wonder how they are organized. Actually, they're appearing in the sequence in which they were initially published on my website, **www.bradgraber.com.** At first I tried to organize them into cogent categories, but that seemed awkward and artificial. So, I decided to let you, the reader, discover each "nugget of wisdom" (I hope you will regard some of them as such!) with a flip of the page. If you really love a piece, I've provided a table of contents to make it easy to find it again.

NOW TO THE TITLE AND COVER.

Admittedly, both are unconventional. Yet there are moments when little annoyances creep into our everyday lives. For me, one such annoyance is symbolized by that container of sour cream. Okay. I'm terrible with expiration dates. What can I say? I'd initially thought of calling the book *You're Born with the Face God Gave You—You Wind Up with the Face You Deserve.* My grandmother often used that expression. She was a lovely woman, yet I'm not sure that observation was meant as a compliment. It probably was a warning to a child who didn't smile enough. Either way. I'll probably use that title for a future book. Yes, I am an ambitious fellow.

happyreading!

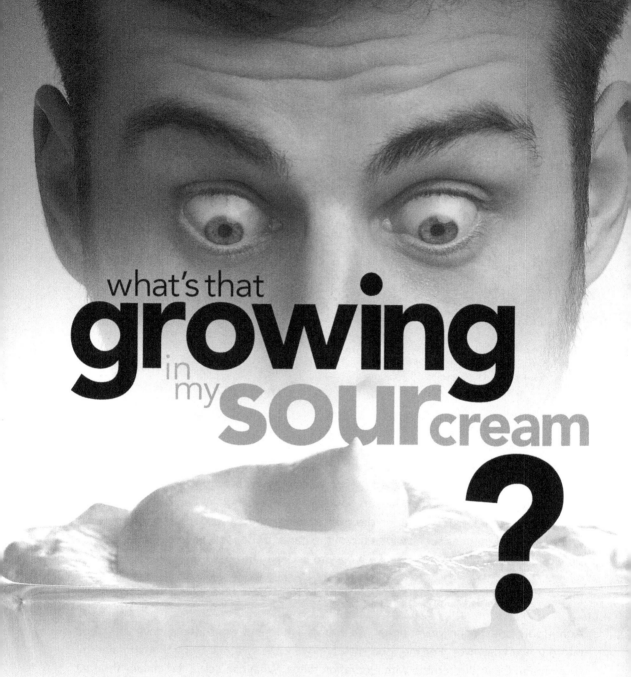

what's that growing in my sour cream?

IN OUR HOUSE, WE HAVE A BAD HABIT.

We keep certain items in the refrigerator far too long. Now, I'm not referring to the ketchup, mustard, relish, and that jar of jelly tucked in the door. When were they purchased? Who knows? They always taste fine. Which makes me wonder, does a condiment ever go bad?

DAIRY

One thing that doesn't hold up as well is dairy. You know when the milk has turned, by the flecks that appear in your coffee. Before plastic containers, I used to think those floating islands were pieces of wax from the carton. Of course, milk's expiration date is front and center when you buy it. It's not unusual to see people buried in the refrigerated section, butts sticking out of the dairy case, searching for the latest expiration date. But then most people use milk every day. The likelihood of its going bad is pretty slim. And if it does, coffee offers that early warning system before the milk is added to the cereal.

SOUR CREAM

Sour cream, on the other hand, is a different dairy story. We don't use it often, but when we do, there's always a half-used container sitting in the refrigerator. And, since I'm the guy who plans most of our meals and hates to waste food, that darn sour cream calls out to me: "How can you use me up today?" I usually have no idea. Until I do.

SURPRISE, SURPRISE

And when you think about it, doesn't sour cream sound as if it has already gone bad? Sure, it does. Which makes its extended stay in the refrigerator even more alarming. I can't tell you—though I'm about to anyway—how often I've peeked in the container and seen something nasty. Something green and fuzzy. Like the art project your kid might bring home from school. Only, with an added aroma.

LIFE

Perhaps sour cream is a metaphor for life! Delicious when it's fresh, not so great when it's old and expired. And it's our job to think about how to use it all up in the most creative way. So, here's to hoping that there's nothing growing in your sour cream. That every day is a bright and happy one. And most important, that your expiration date affords you to do all the wonderful things you love with the people you love. Including eating blintzes, baked potatoes, and Mexican food. Which by the way, all go great with sour cream.

"the
liberation
of marcia brady"

I happened to catch an episode of The Brady Bunch on the very morning that Hillary Clinton was to accept the Democratic nomination for President of the United States.

THAT'S WHAT I DO WHEN I WAKE UP AT 4:30 A.M.

I sit in front of the television with a cup of coffee, blinking hard until the world comes into focus. 1970s sitcom television is about all I can handle. It's my precursor to the morning news. Which by the way, requires another cup of coffee.

The show was titled "The Liberation of Marcia Brady" and was written to address America's growing concern with feminism and women's rights— concepts that galvanized the girls as much as it riled the boys in the Brady household. And even though there was no bra burning or marching, the point was clear: Times were changing. Women were finding their voices. Heck, even Alice and Carol Brady were onboard.

As the episode unfolded, I couldn't help but wonder about the timing of the telecast. Did someone deliberately select that particular morning to air the episode? Could it have just been a coincidence?

THAT SEEMED UNLIKELY.

Watching the show was like opening a time capsule. I was reminded that change comes slowly, if at all. And that each one of us has prejudices to overcome. Prejudices that are reflective of the era in which we're raised.

Oh, sure. We've had other notable female politicians. Who could forget Shirley Chisholm, Bella Abzug, Barbara Jordan, and Geraldine Ferraro, to name but a few? But, as I watched the Brady family that morning, I wondered if America had ever been this close to electing a female president.

Hillary's nomination made me realize how far we've come as a Nation. And despite her loss at the polls in 2016, the glass ceiling is now permanently cracked. We will eventually have a female president. At least, I hope so.

Now it's time for America to get onboard with equal pay for equal work. Marcia, Hillary, and the women of America deserve nothing less.

threerules
to follow

WHEN LAUNCHING
A SECOND CAREER

I KNOW WHAT YOU'RE THINKING.

You don't want a second career. You've worked hard all your life and now all you want to do is chill. Do absolutely nothing. Become a beach bum.

I completely understand.

But, when you retire, there's going to be a moment that you look around and think: What the heck am I going to do with myself today?

Worse yet: What am I going to do tomorrow?

THE CLOCK WILL BECOME AN ARMED-GUARD,

unwilling to let you pass through the endless afternoon. Whenever you look up, it'll be two o'clock. Just like the movie Groundhog Day.

Now how can that be? Wasn't it just two o'clock a few hours ago?

THREE TIPS

So, here are three tips to help you prepare for the big day.

You'll want to make a note of this before you're at the company retirement party, or, worse, as Human Resources walks you out the door. If you're planning on being carried out on a stretcher, your face covered with a sheet, you can stop reading now.

1 SEEK OPPORTUNITIES WITH START-UPS OR NONPROFITS

Why give up thinking just because you prefer to sleep late in the morning?

Before you retire, while you're still employed with that impressive title, explore opportunities with companies that capture your interest. Whether you decide to be a community volunteer, or step into an unpaid consulting role on the board, having some place to go when you retire will be a blessing. And volunteering still allows for plenty of time for tennis and golf.

2 DO WHAT GIVES YOU PLEASURE

Make your daydreams come true. If you've always wanted to paint, sign up for an art course. Go on to Meetup.com to search groups in your area engaged in hobbies from hiking, attending sporting events and lectures, or doing whatever strikes your fancy. Commit to going to at least two events a month for three months. You'll meet new people, and many, just like you, will be looking for structured activities to give balance to their lives. Plus, you'll learn a lot.

3 GO EASY ON YOURSELF

Change is hard. No doubt there will be moments when you feel lost and confused. It happens to the best of us. On those days, recognize that no one is perfect. And, oh yes. Welcome to the club!

assault rifles:

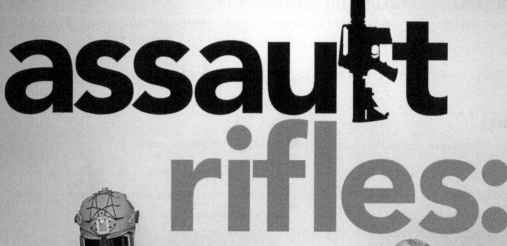

ISN'T THE DANGER RIGHT THERE IN THE NAME?

I'M STUMPED BY THIS.

If I was grocery shopping, and came across a breakfast cereal named *Cancer Corn*, I'd never buy it.

If I was in the market for a new car, I'd pass on an automobile named *A-Bomb*. It's not that I'm a bad driver, but who would want to risk a nuclear event with the simple turn of an ignition key?

If I were in the mood for something sweet, I'd avoid *Jawbreakers*. Mostly because I'm afraid of the dentist, but also because it's impossible to get those things into your mouth without choking.

Yet, in America, military-style *assault* weapons are available to purchase for wild game-hunting and self-protection?

SEEMS LIKE OVER-KILL.

OR AM I MISSING SOMETHING?

tomorrowland

THE OTHER DAY, I HAD THE STRANGEST FEELING —

a keen sense of déjà vu as I stared at my iPhone, checking my Instagram account. I was once again at the 1964 New York World's Fair. Captivated by the modern conveniences showcased at the pavilions of General Electric, Bell Systems, Ford, General Motors, and Westinghouse. Would I ever really see those inventions in my lifetime?

In the 1980s, the desktop computer arrived. Next, the microwave oven—which was okay for reheating foods but not so great for cooking a meal. Then, the CD player: thin discs to replace big LPs.

I remembered seeing these products years before they appeared in the stores. Before there was a Best Buy or Fry's Electronics. Or Amazon. My eight-year-old self wasn't surprised by the technology. Just by how long it took for it to finally arrive in my home. The iPhone. Skype. Texting. Would the world ever really have that kind of connectivity?

The speed of innovation has changed the landscape of our lives. The Kodak Instamatic disappeared. Encyclopedias: gone. The landline telephone, a dinosaur. Televisions morphed from small boxes with five or six channels to flat widescreens with hundreds of channels. PayPal, Bitcoin, and Apple money have emerged. There are even predictions about the disappearance of paper money.

THEN THE SIGHT OF A DRIVERLESS CAR JOLTED ME.

Of course, I remember.

I waited decades—and now that promised world has come into view. It's happened. It's real. It's exciting. And I feel like I did when I was eight years old anticipating the next innovation in Tomorrowland!

elevator pitch:

STUCK BETWEEN THE FLOORS?

GROWING UP IN A NEW YORK CITY HIGH-RISE APARTMENT BUILDING,

I would have thought it a no-brainer for me to come up with an elevator pitch for my novels. A short, pithy, "got you!" hook that would compel thousands to purchase and read my fiction.

AFTER ALL,

I've spent countless hours riding up and down in an elevator—not to mention being stuck between floors—listening to adults swap stories. Recapping the visit of an aunt, the illness of a child, the death of a parent. All done in under a minute or less. The juiciest teasers being spoken just before the elevator doors opened to the next floor.

And yet, every time someone asks me about my fiction, I struggle. I should be able to do a quick recap. Who knows my novels better than I do? How could I possibly have spent all those hours (years, in fact) writing and be unable to quickly describe my own stories?

Perhaps it's because I'm inherently shy. Uncomfortable being on the spot. Or, maybe, I'm reluctant to be judged.

Oh—when you meet me—you don't get that. Hey, I've been an adult for quite a while. I've mastered the art of being friendly and gracious. But inside, truths burn brightly. No matter how you may present yourself, deep down, you know who you are. I'm someone who is much more comfortable writing a blog than talking about his novels.

SO LET'S PRETEND.

We're now riding between floors and you want to know what my novels are about. Get your stopwatch ready. I'm reaching deep. Here we go:

The Intersect: Strangers' lives cross in a heartwarming tale of love and friendship that will leave you wishing these people were part of your family.

After the Fall: A teenager searches for a long-lost uncle in hopes of learning the truth about her mother's mysterious death.

My fiction is about truth, love, and building relationships that endure. It's about finding the mystery of human connection in surprising places. It's what I believe we all yearn for…and fear we will never have.

It's what I hope for everyday in my life. And it's my greatest wish for you.

fighting
with technology

FROM INDIA AND BACK

THE OTHER DAY, MY COMPUTER ROUTER CRASHED. I HADN'T REALIZED THAT IT'S THE HEART OF THE ENTIRE HOME OFFICE.

No router—no phones—no Internet—no Netflix—no printer.Now, I've had problems before with the modem. But that's easily reset. You call the cable company, they magically reset it on their end, and you're up and running again. But when your router doesn't work, it's not such an easy fix, because the cable company doesn't own the router. Which means the router requires a call to a distant land. INDIA.

MODEM VS. ROUTER

Now, don't be fooled. I'm not technically sophisticated. There was a time when I had no idea about the differences between a modem and a router. I eventually figured out that it's important to label both and their respective plugs, since unplugging from the outlet is a critical step to rebooting. Without a label on the plug, it's nearly impossible to sort through the bowl of spaghetti—wires shooting out everywhere—that lies behind my desk. So labeling is especially helpful whenever the system crashes, because that's when I lose my cookies and get easily confused. I know this, because the system tends to go down a lot.

OLDER COMMUNITIES

My cable provider tells me I live in one of those older neighborhoods where something or other needs to be upgraded. Odd—because telephone solicitors have no trouble finding me. Scam artists appear regularly in my electronic mailbox. And Facebook knows more about me than my own mother ever did. I just nod my head and assume that the cable provider must know their business. Still, I can't help but think they are full of hooey.

NOT MY ROUTER!

To be honest, the people who work with me on the phone from India are very kind. They never seem to lose their cool—even as I am stomping about—completely frustrated because I don't always understand what is going on or what they are saying.

It isn't always the accent. Sometimes, it's the techie talk.

Okay. Sometimes it is the accent. Certain words just need to be spelled out. But often, we struggle with the International language of computers that eludes my simian brain. It seems that I have a mental freeze when I look at my screen and have to explain what I'm seeing. It's especially odd that a writer is unable to find the right words. To me, it sometimes feels like trying to describe a Picasso. Impossible to do.

PATIENCE

I can only imagine the difficulty for the poor techie from India. Trying to work over the phone to resolve issues they can't see—and using me as the interpreter.

And so, when I get upset, I try to shift the focus. Make a personal connection. "So, how long have you been doing this job? How do you manage with customers like me who are upset? Have you ever been to America?"

I've discovered that you can learn a lot by talking with kindness. It resets the entire experience. It still takes two hours to get the router fixed—and yes, you're still exasperated at the end—but in a way, you've made the time work for you. You've learned a little bit more about someone you'd never actually meet otherwise.

IN THE END, I FEEL GRATEFUL

One day, I'd like to visit India and meet some of the folks who work in those call centers. I'd like to know what their lives are like and how they find the patience to work these kinds of jobs. Maybe I can pick up a pointer or two for the next time my system goes down. Hmmm. Come to think of it—that could be any minute now.

calling
davidsedaris:

I'M OVER HERE

I'VE OFTEN FANTASIZED

that David Sedaris might agree to provide a blurb for my book because—well—he's David Sedaris, an extremely successful author with a legion of fans. And me? Well, I'm not.

He's such a clever, witty, sophisticated guy that I know he'd enjoy rooting for my characters as they tackle life. I can almost hear him warmly saying, "Brad, your novels are brilliant. I wish I'd written them!"

OVERNIGHT, MY SALES WOULD SKY-ROCKET.

But getting someone famous like Sedaris in my corner might prove a challenge. How many other authors must be competing for his endorsement? I'd bet his home in the Hamptons (I just made that up—I have no idea where he lives) is overrun with unsolicited manuscripts. Stacks everywhere. From cookbooks to contemporary fiction. Voices crying out to be heard: "READ ME. PLEASE READ ME."

SO HOW TO GET HIS ATTENTION?

I could buy a billboard in Times Square sporting the cover of my book and a headline in bright neon—***Calling David Sedaris.***

I could rent the Goodyear Blimp and fly it over the GLBTQ parade in L.A.—assuming he'd be in attendance—with a flowing banner—***Calling David Sedaris.***

I could place an advertisement in ***Publishers Weekly.*** By now, you know how it would read.

Or perhaps I should write a simple letter that I can send through his publisher. Appeal to his kindness…tell him a bit about myself and what inspired me to write…maybe send along a complimentary copy of my novels. Who knows? That just might work.

No. The billboard in Times Square. That's definitely the ticket.

ageism:

LIVE LONG ENOUGH—IT'LL FIND YOU

FOR YEARS,

I've been a volunteer driver for Duet, a nonprofit organization in Phoenix, Arizona, that assists seniors in arranging for transportation to and from their doctor appointments.

MOST OF MY PASSENGERS ARE OLDER WOMEN.

Perhaps they're best at asking for help. Or maybe it's just true that woman tend to outlive men.

The women are invariably happy to share a bit about their lives as we head to a nearby appointment. I'm always struck by their dignity and resolve to carry on when family and friends have moved away, or died, or simply left them to their own devices. I think it takes courage to face life when you're unsure how you'll get to the doctor. I marvel at their resilience and strength. Most have raised families, buried husbands, and some have even buried children, and still they go on with determination and a loving spirit.

One thing is for sure: I have met a lot of lovely ladies in their 80s.

I've always thought I'd be a terrible older person. Crabby, demanding, and ridiculously impatient with myself and everyone else. To be honest, I wasn't so great at being young. Surely, being ill-tempered would be a part of my aging process. But as I view these wonderful and unique individuals, I see a sparkle in their eyes as they embrace life. And I find myself thinking: "perhaps I just might make a delightful older man. Someone who attracts people. Someone who astounds strangers with his positive attitude".

And then I realize, it's simply ageist to think getting older turns you into Ebenezer Scrooge.

I could still have another good thirty years. I might end up alone, no family or friends around. It could happen. So, I'd better start practicing being kind and loving. I'll definitely need those skills when someone from Duet drives me to my doctor's appointment. That, and patience as the driver circles the parking lot, trying to find the closest spot to the medical building's front door.

why burn

the garlictoast...

WHEN YOU CAN JUST AS EASILY POISON YOUR DINNER GUESTS?

It seems my spouse and I are unable to manage a simple dinner party for six without burning something.

THE OTHER NIGHT, IT WAS THE GARLIC BREAD.

I had made lasagna and a salad. Even baked a cake. Friends had gathered. Ella (Fitzgerald) was singing softly in the background. The lights were dim. Everyone and everything seemed perfect, as it always does when the lights are low.

People were mingling and laughing. I was happy. A glass of red wine in my hand and things were smoothly under way. We were moments away from sitting down at the table, and even with one oven, I'd managed to pull together a great meal.

IT WAS QUITE A RELIEF.

You see, for me, entertaining at home isn't exactly a joy. There's no Ina Garten or Giada in my kitchen. It's more—Fred Willard meets The Gong Show (forgive me for the dated references, but that's just how I roll).

First, I have to check all the expiration dates. If you don't cook a lot, Costco may not be the ideal place to shop. Fearful of poisoning friends, I pitch anything that seems too old, but not after a lot of back and forth wondering whether it really matters if you are within six to eight months of an expiration date. Sadly, that happens a lot. But good sense prevails. I always toss.

I also hate cooking. Some people find it relaxing. I think there should be a special lockdown unit for those folks. All I ever see is a mounting pile of dirty pots and pans. I've even become an expert at using tin foil to line everything to ease the clean-up. Still, someone has to wipe the counters and put every-thing away.

So, it's not that I'm inhospitable—it's just a lot of work.

You have to make sure the house is clean, especially the guest bathroom, and though we hardly ever use it, for some reason, it's always dirty. Then you have to clean up outside. Not that you'll be sitting out there, but in Arizona the outside patio is plainly seen from every window—even at night, because we have special outdoor lights that illuminate the exterior. Sometimes I find myself measuring the value of a friendship in direct correlation to the amount of work required to clean up.

Love my friends. Hate to clean up.

So, there we were. Enjoying a great beginning until I decided to crisp up the garlic bread. Just slide it under the broiler for a minute or two. Great idea. But with the wine in hand, a friend talking to me, the minute became longer—and before I realized it—the kitchen filled with smoke.

SUCCESSFUL DINNER PARTIES? MY ADVICE. ORDER IN.

facebook
friendships:

REALLY?

OKAY. I ADMIT IT.

I WAS AT A HOLIDAY PARTY AND EXCITED TO SEE TWO FRIENDS.

As I rushed over to talk with them, it occurred to me that they were, at best, acquaintances of mine. My exuberance hardly matched the level of the friendship. So how could I feel so close to people who were really just acquaintances?

ONE WORD. *FACEBOOK*

WE'D BEEN FACEBOOK FRIENDS FOR A FEW WEEKS,

and whether it's the holiday season or just that time of year, these Facebook friends had been posting a lot about their history. When they met. Photos of what they looked like thirty years ago. Where they lived. I'd even become familiar with their pets, past and present.

And then came Throwback Thursdays. That's when I learned that one of the couple had experienced a serious bout with cancer years earlier.

The postings had become so personal and moving—like a good book—I'd been completely drawn in. Maybe a bit too much.

I immediately became wary.

Do people who read my novels assume they have an intimate knowledge of me?

I write contemporary fiction—not memoir—and though you write best when you "write what you know," my novels aren't autobiographical. Details are stretched, words polished, intentions shaped, and still, friends try to guess which character is me and how much of the novel is true.

Interestingly enough, I'm never the teenager or the older woman in the story. I'm always an age-appropriate, male character. Which is odd, because I've really giving birth to every character. They're all me.

Perhaps privacy for an author is really just an illusion.

That said, I've rarely had anyone come up to me at a party as if I were a long-lost friend. But then, I don't have a huge number of Facebook followers. Which raises the question: How many followers does one need to feel connected to the outside world?

Perhaps Facebook does serve a purpose. It just might be the literature of the masses. Instead of reading a good book, people are busy reading about someone else's life. Posts become scenes. Pics, the new chapter headings. And everyone is an author of their own story. Perhaps that's why it makes for such good reading.

Or just maybe, we've all become lazy, and investing time in reading a good book has become a luxury. Perhaps in the future, smart authors will be posting new scenes on Facebook.

Hmm. Now there's a **novel** idea.

betrayed
by a
fortune
cookie

LAST SATURDAY, WE HAD LUNCH AT A LOCAL CHINESE RESTAURANT IN MY HOMETOWN OF PHOENIX.

Being born and raised in New York City, and after living in San Francisco for ten years, I find there tends to be a difference in style between the two coasts when it comes to the preparation of Chinese cuisine. Luckily, in Phoenix you can find Chinese food that caters to either palate.

East Coast Chinese tends to be Americanized—chow mein, egg foo yung, heavy sauces, crispy noodles, sweet and sour everything.

West Coast tends to be lighter, with lots of fresh seafood options and gentle flavors.

East Coast reminds me of my childhood—West Coast—my once insurmountable Mill Valley, California, mortgage. But both coasts share one thing in common. The check always arrives with a fortune cookie.

Though once disputed by the Hong Kong Noodle Company in Los Angeles, the courts found in 1983 that the fortune cookie was an early invention of a San Francisco bakery. Should you journey to San Francisco, you can see the cookies being made at the Golden Gate Fortune Cookie Factory—part of a walking tour that includes Chinatown.

So there we were at China Chili (East Coast style) in Phoenix. The meal was all but consumed when along came the check. We both reached for our fortune cookies. Jeff, my husband, read his aloud. Typical fortune about a bright future. I opened mine and stared at the slip of paper.

"Faith answered. No one was there."

I've heard of a bad meal but not a bad fortune cookie. I almost insisted on a do-over as I watched Jeff fall apart with laughter.

Now I realize a writer needs more than faith to be successful. But somewhere in the recesses of my brain I'd thought that faith in my future success would be an advantage.

Next time, I think I'll ask for the almond cookie.

going **white** in the age of **trump**

I DON'T KNOW WHAT GOT INTO ME, BUT THE OTHER DAY AT THE DENTIST, I AGREED TO HAVE MY TEETH WHITENED.

Maybe it was the dingy color—a recent birthday—or the fact that I haven't ever had my teeth professionally whitened. And, as with all things undertaken spontaneously, I soon came to regret the decision.

WHY?

For people with big smiles and large mouths, tooth whitening really makes sense. After all, everyone can see their teeth. But for someone like me, who has a small mouth and rarely smiles, what's the point?

As for my husband Jeff, well, he has teeth the size of Chiclets. When he smiles, which he does a lot, the world lights up. I can always tell how our relationship is going based on how often I get to see those teeth. Sometimes, it's not very often.

YOW!

They promised me it wouldn't hurt. Oh sure, they said some people have sensitivity afterward. But I thought they meant when you eat. I hadn't realized my teeth would be twinging and zinging—aching—with sudden shooting pain as if I needed a root canal.

And I hadn't expected the sensitivity to last all day.

LUCKY, I GUESS

So, it seems I'm one of those people with extreme sensitivity. Heck, I am a sensitive kind of guy.

I certainly didn't mind reclining for an hour as my mind ticked through all my real and imagined problems. It was nice to close my eyes in the middle of the day. And then I remembered reading somewhere that when you look at someone's teeth, you've just peeked at their corpse.

HMM. NOW *THAT'S* SOMETHING TO THINK ABOUT.

is that a

birthday
cake

OR A BONFIRE?

As another birthday comes and goes, I've been thinking about the cultural values that we Americans share on aging.

RETIREMENT

Financial planners build their careers tapping into the promise of a secure, happy retirement. Exciting travel. Leisure time with the ones you love. All very enticing—and yet, no one really wants to grow old. That's okay for wine and cheese. But people? Not so much.

GOLF ANYONE?

I think retirement has been romanticized.

Now, I'll admit there's something wonderful about having the day to yourself. Golf, tennis, and hiking—assuming your knees and hips hold out. Walks in the fresh air—if you're steady on your feet and it isn't an ozone watch-day.

Checking out a promotional flier for an adult community reveals happy seniors engaged in water volleyball, dancing, and yoga. When you actually visit, most are sitting around playing cards and complaining. Wait—my mistake. No one plays cards anymore.

YOGA—REALLY?

My biggest concern about aging is staying mentally sharp. I want to continue to learn. Solve problems. And I don't mean what to defrost for dinner.

And though I still enjoy working out—and do it often—I've come to respect the reality of what my body will and will not do. To those who advocate "no pain, no gain," I say "weeks of physical therapy and chiropractic visits!"

A MINDFUL PLAN

I've heard it said that the fastest route to depression is spending too much time focused on yourself. If you want to be truly happy, expand your horizons. Facing an empty day might be a real mood-killer.

SO HOW OLD IS OLD?

"Old" is not a number—it's a mindset. So be old enough to do what you want—and young enough to have something to do.

did anyone **pack?** the **pepto-bismol**

I ALWAYS THINK OF PEPTO-BISMOL AS BEING MOSTLY FOR KIDS.

What other medication comes in bubble-gum pink? Well, I guess there is calamine lotion for poison ivy. But it seems to me that no one over the age of twelve ever really needs Pepto-Bismol. Antacids? Yes. Stool softener? Maybe. Aspirin? Definitely. But, as I've come to learn during a trip to Asia, if you travel overseas, it's always wise to pack the Pepto-Bismol.

PINK?

And in our gender-sensitive world, I'm surprised the pink color has stuck. Pink might be okay for Sally, but shouldn't Billy's version be blue? Which reminds me of something silly that Phyllis Schlafly (remember her?) might have said in the 1960s defending her opposition to the Equal Rights Amendment. After all, she viewed gender in very specific terms.

ARE THOSE PEPPERS?

So, there we were in Vietnam. Far away from home. About to consume a wonderful meal in a local Vietnamese restaurant. And, without thinking, I poured hot sauce into my fish pho. That's a beef bouillon soup with a lot of noodles topped with fried fish sticks (hey, I'm just trying to get the imagery; if you want accuracy, consult the Iron Chef). Error number two? My first spoonful included a hot pepper. My mouth, eyes, and gut were instantly on fire.

NOTHING GOOD COMES FROM FLAMING GUTS

The next day, it wasn't pretty. It was as if I'd begun a colonoscopy prep. Far, far off, in a distant land where the people are gentle and kind, I was eliminating toxic waste. Hadn't America already done enough to Vietnam? Did I also have to leave my mark?

THINK TWICE NEXT TIME

And so, that very afternoon, I came to realize the value of Pepto-Bismol. A wonder drug, indeed. And though I hadn't packed it, a friend had, and, being kind, shared the mother lode with me.

So, I've learned my lesson. Next time I travel overseas I'll be ready.

CALAMINE LOTION ANYONE?

my newcar

_____

IS UP ON THE ROOF

_____

I'M ONE OF THOSE PEOPLE WHO HATES TO BUY A NEW CAR.

The truth is, I don't like spending large sums of money on myself. On my husband, sure. On the dog, let's do it. On me—not so much.

LEASE

I'm far too practical to lease. I tend to buy and hold, fully depreciating the investment. Plus, leasing would require that I walk into a showroom every few years and make another selection. I don't like showrooms. The sales staff are way too attentive. Asking all sorts of personal questions and offering coffee at every turn. I wouldn't mind a large glazed donut—but the baked goods are usually reserved for the suckers getting their cars serviced. Jiffy Lube doesn't serve food. Now you know where I hang out for service.

CAR-BLIND

A friend of mine who works for General Motors recently told me I had lousy taste in cars. I should be offended, but in truth, all cars look alike to me. Yes. I can tell an SUV from a sedan. A sports car from a luxury model. I'm not stupid. I just can't tell one SUV from another. Inside and out, they all seem the same. Which makes finding my SUV in any parking lot a real challenge.

DETROIT CAR SHOW

You'd think after living in Detroit for eighteen years, I'd have developed a real passion for cars.

Well, I haven't.

When I lived in Michigan, I often attended the North American International Auto Show. That's big in Detroit. I remember it well since it was always held in January and so darn cold outside (it's since been moved to June). The cars—well, they left little impression. The new models were frequently showcased on spinning platforms. Between the bright lights, blaring music, new car shine, and large crowds, the whole experience left me dizzy and exhausted.

EIGHT-YEAR MARK

So why am I concerned about a new car? Well, I'm at the eight-year mark. We all know that sooner or later things will go south. My father told me that. So, I've started to shop—which explains all the voice messages on my iPhone. Friends and family text, while car salespeople call. Day and night. Week after week. Seems I've become very popular!

And then, one of our HVACs in the house died. A few days later, in a symbolic show of unity, the other HVAC let out a death rattle. Curing the problem has been an expensive proposition.

So now, my "new car" is up on the roof. That's where the HVAC units sit. I have no idea why the HVACs are up there. I'm just grateful I didn't have to test-drive them.

exercise—

DOES IT REALLY HELP?

I CAN'T FIGURE OUT WHY I'VE BEEN FEELING SO WELL LATELY.

It's not like me to be without an ache or pain. Not that I'm so very old, but I've come to expect sore muscles in the morning. It's kind of routine.

EATING RIGHT?

We just came off a cruise ship. Four-course meals were the rule. The bread-basket at our table was often refilled twice. I became very close with the sourdough. And afterward, there were chocolate chip cookies everywhere. Many were in my hand—before magically disappearing.

WEIGHT LIFTING

I usually go to the gym a couple of times a week, but on the ship, I let that routine go. It's dangerous to work out with all that rocking motion. Experts (don't ask me who) agree that dizziness can cause a sudden fall. I saw no sense risking a broken bone. I'm sure you'd agree.

ELLIPTICAL

Surprisingly, I didn't miss those long sessions on the elliptical machine. Or peddling, peddling, peddling on the stationary bicycle, going nowhere, sweat soaking through my workout clothes. People were just friendlier onboard the ship than when I walk into Trader Joe's following an intense workout before I go home to shower. No one cleared a path, stepped away, or gave me any sense that something was terribly wrong. In short, I smelled fantastic.

NO BACKACHE

Since I've stopped exercising, my back and feet feel terrific! That must be because of the dog. We usually go on long walks together. But he wasn't able to make the trip. Actually, he wasn't invited. But don't feel bad for him. He's having a wonderful week with a great pet sitter. No doubt, he's somewhere now walking his little paws off.

VIC AND JACK

Which leads me to wonder about the true virtues of diet and exercise. Could Vic Tanny, Jack LaLanne, Weight Watchers, and Pritikin all have it wrong? Have we been sold a bill of goods by the health & wellness Industry? Could excessive eating and a lack of exercise actually be good for you?

It's only been a few days since I was relaxing on board the ship, and yet I can't stop thinking about all the professional athletes on dry land who are soaking somewhere in an ice bath to relieve the pain. Or those weekend warriors straining into the next stretch. I wish them all, wherever they are, a big basket of hot sourdough bread—plus some real butter—and maybe a chocolate chip cookie thrown in for good measure.

HAPPY

hour
anyone?

I'VE BEGUN TO NOTICE THAT MY THIRTEEN-YEAR-OLD DOG IS EATING EARLIER AND EARLIER.

He used to eat dinner at 5:00 p.m., but over the last few weeks, after his insistent whining and vocalizing, we've moved dinner time to 4 o'clock.

WHO COULD STAND THE CRYING?

So, what's the big deal? Who cares when the dog eats? Certainly not me. Frankly, I wouldn't mind eating dinner at 4:00 p.m. but I've been told that I'm too young for that. Only the elderly eat so early. And since I certainly don't want to be judged as elderly, I shrug and go along.

BUT I'M HUNGRY!

So, what I'd really like to know is—what does *age* have to do with the time of day when you eat? Someone please answer me that! Besides, it turns out that 4:00 p.m. is now designated as Happy Hour. A chic, sophisticated concept, created by the hospitality industry. Discounted bites and liquor. I'm sure you've heard of it. It's the time when adults gather in the late afternoon to drink. A prelude, if you will, to the real show—that little thing I call dinner.

TEETOTALER

I don't really drink. Maybe a martini now and then. A glass of wine, to be polite among company. Champagne on special occasions. But generally, drinking just isn't *my thing*. Yet Phoenix is ripe with all sorts of restaurants catering to the Happy Hour concept. I suspect more than one cheapskate has figured out that loading up on discounted food will certainly stretch the social security check. But when we go, I don't see older folks. No walkers or canes. No wheelchairs. Only young hipsters—and upscale adults—gathering about, smartly dressed, engaged in what may be witty repartee. The food seems to be of secondary importance. The focus is on the drinks.

LIVE MUSIC SO I CAN'T HEAR MYSELF CHEW

The way I see it, Happy Hour is a perfect excuse for moving mealtime to 4 o'clock. No one seems to notice that I'm even eating. They're all too busy "oohing" and "ahhing" over this or that novelty cocktail while I'm busy eyeing the food—trying to determine how many small plates I need to create a decent-sized meal.

You can't fool me. Happy Hour is just the modern version of an Early Bird Special. Let the others drink to their hearts' content. I'm eating dinner.

white
tube
socks

I'VE BEEN TOLD THAT WEARING WHITE TUBE SOCKS IS PASSÉ.

And if the crowd at the gym is any indication, that's certainly true. Black is the new white. So, I bought some black no-show socks—the short ones you can't see when you put on your sneakers. And I gathered up all my old white tube socks with the intent of sending them to a friend who said he uses them when he dusts. Sock puppets, I get. Dusting? Not so much.

SLIPPAGE

No sooner was I on the elliptical at the gym than one of my new socks started to slip. Halfway through my workout, it had crept down to the bottom of my foot, eventually balling up under my heel.

DON'T REACH DOWN?

There have been moments when I've nearly lost my balance on the elliptical due to a minor distraction. Straining to make out a CNN headline on the flat-screen television mounted high above the gym. Spotting an attractive passerby and allowing my eye to linger too long. Listening to Eydie Gormé on my iPod. She may be dead and buried but she can sure as hell belt out a tune. Swinging your arms to and fro as she hits a high note can be dangerous. It's best to listen from a seated position.

SAFETY FIRST

So, I waited till the workout was over and headed to the locker room to remove my sneaker and that pesky sock. That's when I noticed the residue: black fuzz buried deep in the corner of my toenail. Not a good look. So I decided to keep the white tube socks. I mean, really! Who cares what I wear on my feet when I work out? It's no one else's business. Besides, ankle-high white tube socks look so darn good with summer sandals.

"what?"
did you say

I'VE BEEN DEAF IN MY LEFT EAR SINCE I WAS TWO YEARS OLD.

Pneumonia. Dead nerve. Nothing they could do about it. At least until cochlear implants came along. But honestly, I'm not interested in the procedure. After all these years, I'm kind of used to not hearing on my left side.

I'M CHANGE ADVERSE

While everyone wants the latest and greatest, I'm usually bemoaning the loss of the familiar. Now, there are some things I don't miss. Black-and-white television. The flip phone. TV dinners (okay—I might actually miss those; but have you checked the salt content?). And really, I don't miss the hearing I never had.

GROWING UP

The New York City school system required me to have my hearing tested each year. I'd sit in a soundproof booth as the audiologist turned up the volume to a roar. I couldn't hear a thing in my left ear, but I did feel the pressure on my eardrum. That's when I'd raise my hand and they'd stop.

And because I had years of lip-reading classes and no discernible speech challenges, people don't always remember that I have a handicap. Teachers walked about the room during spelling tests. It was impossible for me to hear them. So, I figured out a work-around: I learned the week's words…memorizing the list…and filled in the blanks at the end of the spelling test…those words I'd missed. That always surprised the teacher. Hey, what can I say? You do what you need to do to get by.

YOU LEARN TO OVERCOMPENSATE

Throughout my business career, I suffered through many round-conference-table meetings. I learned early on that it was best to be upfront with the neighbor on my left. I'd turn to the person and explain that I couldn't hear on that side. Invariably, that person would engage me in a long discussion. Of course, I could only catch a word or two. Something about a relative with the same condition. I'd smile and hope they'd stop talking. Very awkward. Or during the lunch portion of the meeting, they would ask for the salt. A lot of people on my left always seemed to want the salt.

"BUT I DIDN'T *HEAR* YOU"

And then there were the people who thought I was just unfriendly. Stuck up. Too good to talk to them. That happened a lot. If you were standing on my left side, I just wouldn't know that you were talking to me. And no, peripheral vision doesn't offset for a hearing loss. Hey, we all have our moments, but in a large room with lots of background noise, I'm never going to hear clearly. Close friends know that. Now, so do you, the next time you're at one of my book-signings.

HAVE I MISSED THE HEARING?

I still have one reasonably good ear. And, based on my life experience, I don't think I've missed much. Those who've wanted to make their points known—partners, family, friends, and even a few therapists—have been heard. Others, who filled the air with noise, mean talk, or cutting criticism, still ring in my "good" ear. At times, I'm even grateful for my handicap. When you're partially deaf, you learn to listen very carefully. That helps decipher what's truly important. And if all else fails…well…you can always pass the salt.

let's eat

I'VE BEEN THINKING A LOT LATELY ABOUT EATING.

Well, I'm on a cruise ship circling Australia—and frankly, eating is the major activity. And despite what you might have heard about Americans' being overweight, I assure you, we're not alone. There are plenty of people from Australia and the UK on board who easily match us in girth. Perhaps that's because taking a cruise is a way of self-selecting those who are obsessively interested in dining as they float along to the next destination.

GROUP-THINK

Food seems to be on everyone's mind. What you ate, what you're eating, what you're going to eat. And instead of being pleasurable, it becomes a little sickening. Especially when you wolf down two hot dogs and fries with a pizza chaser (guilty!). Can the second ice cream sundae be too far behind? Are those chocolate chip or peanut butter cookies? I didn't know Jell-O and cheesecake worked so well together.

I've tried my best not to give into the mass hysteria that the next meal might be our last. And yet, even as I sit here, content to spill my guts about the incredible excesses everywhere, I'm pondering the sugar donuts I saw at the buffet. I should have eaten one of those when I had the chance. Will there be any left if I go back?

AM I SHOWING?

Each morning I awake and stare at my gut in the mirror of my shipboard bath-room. As I stroke my belly, I wonder if it's getting bigger. I'm reminded of that guy Morgan Spurlock who did the *Super Size Me* documentary. You remember him? He ate McDonald's every day for a month to determine the impact on his overall health. As I recall, he got pretty sick. Even vomited. The thought has crossed my mind. Instead, I keep popping antacid after antacid.

I wish I had more self-control. But I don't. Day three and food is everywhere. Except at the gym. And yes, I've actually been there. But any plan to stay slim is 80 percent diet—20 percent exercise. That's what I've heard. So really, there's little point going to the gym while on board. Unless you plan to lie on your back, mouth closed, to ease digestion.

NO MORE

I've told Jeff that this is the last time we go on a cruise. Our next vacation will be an active one. Bicycling through the French countryside. Hiking in California. Rafting down the Colorado River. He agreed with me as we sat in the dining room admiring the sweet rolls placed table-side by the waiter. And as I bit into a fresh croissant with a chocolate center, I realized that this moment won't last forever. Soon, I'll be back at my house where carbs are banned. Where the evenings are spent foraging through cupboards that hold nothing more than spices and dried beans. My stomach will once again be flat. My persistent indigestion: gone.

I guess sometimes in life we just need to *let go*. Practicing self-control on a cruise ship is a fool's journey. Better to fully immerse oneself and get it out of your system. And so, once again I prepare for breakfast. Did you know that pancakes taste best when covered yea-high in stewed prunes?

aussie
survivor

EVER HIKE AN AUSTRALIAN PRESERVE IN SEARCH OF
WILD ANIMALS? ME NEITHER. AT LEAST,
NOT UNTIL THE OTHER DAY.

IT WAS A SIDE TRIP RECOMMENDED BY FRIENDS.

I went along with it mostly because Jeff had always wanted to go on an African safari. So, this was my concession. Instead of days out in the wilderness living off the land, it would be just a couple of hours in a preserve riding around in a Mercedes van with a group of strangers and a very nice tour guide.

It turned out to be a day-long excursion that lasted from 11:00 in the morning until 10:30 at night. A stretch of time that included two meals and what generally passes for my bedtime. Of course, my greatest concerns were: What would we eat, and where would we find a restroom?

NYC CHILDHOOD

Growing up in New York City, I'm not much for wild animals. Oh—we had our native species of cockroach. Two-inch long brown water bugs with cellophane-like wings. And then there was that occasional mouse. It generated a lot of excitement when it showed up. But I don't remember anyone running for a camera.

Pigeons lined the terraces, which we rarely used. And just like an episode from Marlin Perkins's *Wild Kingdom*, some even attempted to nest, until brooms were pulled out to sweep them away. The adults called the pigeons "rats with wings," and years later, on a trip to Venice, I thought a lot about that reference as they swooped overhead in St. Mark's Square.

NO PETS, PLEASE

Dogs and cats were barred from our building when I was growing up. And now that I think of it, I didn't have a single friend back then who owned a pet. Not a bird, turtle, or hamster. Not even a goldfish. So, as I marched through the Aussie forest preserve, with damp leaves, broken sticks, and loose rocks underfoot, I barely looked up from the trail, hoping that I wouldn't be the first to slip and fall into the deep canyon below. All the while, our guide kept yammering. "There are twenty varieties of snakes here. Poisonous spiders that are perfectly camouflaged to match the bark. Kangaroos that have been known to injure dogs." I kept thinking, *and why am I searching for all that?*

UH-OH

And then, up ahead, resting in a tree—a Koala bear! Gray and fuzzy, with Mickey Mouse ears and enormous eyes. He stared down at us as we stared back up at him. I forgot about the dangers, the dampness, and all that dung underfoot. I was part of nature, enjoying the moment, and grateful to be on the trip.

We spotted kangaroos by the dozens, wombats, wallabies, possums, birds of every stripe and color. And though I can't really say that I saw a new career blossoming in wildlife ecology, I learned an important lesson: Even a New York City kid can overcome his rigid nature by being surrounded by nature. I'm now even considering renting that movie with Meryl Streep. What was it called? Oh, yes. *Out of Africa.*

now i
laymedown

I JUST RECEIVED ANOTHER INVITATION FROM THE NATIONAL CREMATION SOCIETY.

They seem to be reaching out to me monthly. They must know something I don't. Perhaps it's the actuarial table for men over sixty.

DIET IS IMPORTANT

A few years back, I rubbed shoulders socially with an oncologist from MD Anderson. We talked about the benefits of eating organic. He made it clear that, for someone my age, it was too late to reap the benefits of an organic diet. I was already filled to the brim with harmful chemicals from a lifetime of processed foods. Thank you, Hostess, Swanson, and Sara Lee. At least now I don't have to feel guilty about *not shopping* at Whole Foods.

PRESCRIPTIONS

At last check, I take no medications. My dad didn't, either, and he bragged about it for years. Then at seventy-eight, he developed a degenerative disease. So much for his "good health." But I did have one grandfather who lived independently into his 90s. He never held an emotion back. He yelled as easily as he cried. He exhausted all of us. And, on reflection, I now wonder if he lived independently because no one could stand his company. That's a sobering thought.

TO BE OR NOT TO BE

In our house, we've discussed whether to be buried or cremated. Jeff wants to be environmentally friendly. He got the idea from living in the Bay Area. I, however, own a plot in Miami. *Of course* I do. Isn't that where all old Jews go to meet their maker? God's waiting room? Most go there while they're still alive to enjoy the sun and ocean. Not me. I wouldn't be caught dead in Florida. Well, actually, one day I will.

And, since I come from a dramatic family, the whole event has been planned out in my mind. Since my family never attends funerals—don't ask me why, but it's a fact—I'll probably prearrange to pay for official mourners. I'll want a lot of tears. And at a key moment in the eulogy, a mourner will cry out, "It should have been me! Why wasn't it me?" Trust me. You won't want to miss it.

BURN, BABY, BURN

In my opinion, dying is sad enough without tossing what remains into the fire. Like the final scene of Citizen Kane where they discover the true meaning of Kane's last word—"*Rosebud.*" No, thank you. And even though I'm not a fan of a deep, dark hole in the ground, I do understand that it's sanitary. Hey, I didn't earn a B.A. in biology for nothing.

ON A FLIGHT TO MEXICO,

sitting in an aisle seat, a passing stranger who was boarding stopped and placed a hand on my shoulder. "Cheer up, buddy," he said. "Things will get better."

Walking the dog in the morning, I've been told by neighbors that I'm rather standoffish.

Friends recently gave me a T-shirt with an imprint of *Grumpy Old Man*.

Other friends gave me a shirt saying: *Everything Hurts and I'm Dying*.

Okay. I've come to accept it. I must seem to be naturally unhappy. Even though that couldn't be further from the truth. Inside, I'm practically exuberant. Well, maybe that's a stretch. How about "content"?

UNFORTUNATE RESTING FACE?

This explains my every childhood photograph. Barely a smile anywhere. Because smiling doesn't come naturally to me. I know, that seems impossible. Then think of Victorian England. Turn-of-the-century America. The Amish. Any cover of Time magazine. No smiles.

KODAK

I believe smiles are a Kodak invention. Not real life.

People don't usually run around with a ridiculous grin. I doubt I'm the only one who has suffered through a family photo session when the photographer has yelled, "Hey, you. The one on the end. How about a smile?"

My facial muscles just don't work that way. Try as I might, I can't achieve a natural smile on demand. I've tried practicing in the mirror. It's impossible.

KINDNESS

So, the next time you see someone with an unhappy expression, consider that they may not know the look they're putting out to the world. Offer them a bright, cheery hello. But for goodness' sake, if it's 6:00 a.m. and they're walking the dog, don't expect them to actually talk. You know—there's only so much anyone can stand in the morning.

but ♡ darling,

I LOVE TURNER CLASSIC MOVIES

I ADMIT IT. I'M ADDICTED TO OLD MOVIES. REALLY, REALLY OLD MOVIES.

I love silent films. I'm fascinated by those stars who never made the transition to sound. John Gilbert. Theda Bara. The list goes on. And though I regularly support the San Francisco Silent Film Festival, I don't always go. But I always want to.

I ALSO LOVE THE EARLY TALKIES.

There's something magical about the films of the 1930s and 1940s. The artistry is amazing. The camera work, the story lines, the actors. But, as with everything in life, even movies made during the Golden Age of Hollywood can be stinkers. Bad directors, bad scripts, bad casting. Just bad movies.

AND THEN, THOSE DATED EXPRESSIONS

Some of the dialogue can be a bit much. Overly dramatic. For instance, the word *darling* pops up an awful lot in love scenes. It's kind of a standard. My grandmother used to call me *"Darling."* But there was never any romantic intent. At least, I don't think so.

I have one friend who uses *darling*. It's a cue that a nasty zinger is about to be hurled your way. If you wear a bathing suit in his presence you might hear, "But *darling*, I thought you worked out." Ouch. He's truly a laugh riot, though you need to have a sense of humor to enjoy it. Fortunately, I do.

OLD HOLLYWOOD

Bette Davis gushed *"darling"* quite a bit in *Now, Voyager*. The Gabor sisters knew how to work a *"darling"* to their advantage. Yet that was more of a Budapest–Green Acres *"dahling."* Tallulah Bankhead was famous for starting nearly every sentence with *"darling."* Check out Hitchcock's *Lifeboat* if you don't believe me. They must have added it into the script just for her.

LONELY GUY

Jeff won't have any part of these older films. I've tried to get him to watch—but the dialogue just turns him right off—even though Bogart, Cagney, Gable, Cooper or Tracy, rarely uttered such nonsense. And so, when my remote somehow locks onto Turner Classic Movies, Jeff tends to rush right out of the room.

I've come to accept it.

Now, I simply yell out, "But *darling*, don't leave me. I can't live without you!"

not another super market

I'VE BEEN THINKING A LOT LATELY ABOUT WHY I SEEM TO ALWAYS BE IN THE SUPERMARKET.

I must have better things to do with my time than wander through Safeway, Fry's, and Trader Joe's. There was a time when I went outside on a nice day and rode a bicycle. Now, I wander the supermarket aisles. Not exactly exercise, but it is walking. Has grocery shopping become my new obsession? Otherwise, how can I explain pushing a shopping cart up and down the grocery aisles every day and thinking that it's fun?

FEED ME

Maybe, it's more about eating. Let's face it. As you age, time is just running out. I suppose the pressure is on to taste everything. Lord knows there's enough food in our house to last for weeks. If we really needed to eat our way through the cabinets, we could easily manage. Though we'd be light on dairy and produce. Plenty of carbs, though.

IS ANYONE ELSE HUNGRY?

Perhaps this is just the result of my upbringing. In my family, food was love. If you cared about someone, you wanted them to eat something delicious. Feeling blue? Have some chocolate pudding. Sick? We have chicken soup for you. Tired? Coffee cake is on its way.

AND BIGGER IS BETTER!

Of course, I'm writing this piece outside Costco waiting for the doors to open. It seems my desire to be entertained has morphed into big-box food stores. Making my second meal of the day on bits of cheese, guacamole dip, and hot appetizers prepared for eager shoppers. I might buy the paper towels, but let's get real. I'm here for the freebies. Snacks on the go!

WORRIED

I try not to let all this food shopping bother me, but I'm getting concerned. I wonder how many other people are feeling trapped by this food fascination. Perhaps it's all just a big nothing. Or maybe I'm onto something. Either way, I find myself totally enraptured. Cut it, slice it, and serve it. I'm there!

who is that
coughing?

I HATE GETTING SICK. I GUESS THAT'S NORMAL.

But I hate it even more when Jeff gets sick. And not because he's desperately ill—or I need to take care of him—but because I'm usually the next one up. It seems when you live with someone it's impossible not to catch their cooties. Especially if you're together working out of the same house.

NOW FOR THE SECRET TO STAYING HEALTHY

Avoid touching your eyes, nose, or mouth. Yeah, right! Like I could ever do that for a solid week. And washing your hands obsessively doesn't help, either. Trust me. I've tried that route, too.

Clorox wipes with bleach are great for killing germs on countertops—but probably not a good idea for wiping down the person lying in bed next to you. Besides, whatever nastiness is happening isn't on the surface. The gross crud is breeding in the recesses of your beloved's nasal cavity, throat, and chest. And sometimes, their tummies.

FLYING

There's nothing worse than being on a plane and hearing someone sneeze. It's like shaking a can of soda and quickly popping it open. You're trapped in a metal cylinder as germs float throughout the cabin. It's impossible to avoid inhaling that wet spray.

And if you must go to the restroom, I recommend washing your hands when you're done and then using a tissue to manage the door handle. God only knows who was in the restroom before you—and there's little doubt what they were doing. Based on my years of observation, men do not always wash their hands after they've done their business. Especially after using a urinal. So, what hope do we have that on a plane they might "discover" the soap and hot water?

BUT I LOVE THE AISLE SEAT

I've read somewhere that the aisle seat is the worst for germ exposure. When boarding, everyone passes by, breathing down on you. And you thought all those knapsacks coming at your head were the problem. Or the wide-hipped flight attendant who keeps knocking into you. Or that damn cart that comes flying down the aisle aimed at your elbow. Really? Is the extra legroom worth it?

CROWDED THEATERS?

I've noticed there's always someone coughing during a play. Probably because plays generally offer a quieter setting. You're straining to hear the lines. Instead, you might hear someone clearing their throat. Sneezing. Snorting. Belching. At the symphony or the opera, it certainly is harder to hear such disturbances. Luckily, in a movie theater, the volume is so loud, it drowns out any background noise. It's impossible to know if anyone nearby is sick. My advice: Slink down into your seat and cover your popcorn with your hand.

COMPASSION

Back in your own household, I think it's best when your spouse is ill to move them into the guest room. Close enough to check on them, but not so close as to be infected. But, of course, the time you spend apart will be dependent on how attracted you are to someone who is needy. Personally, I'm a sucker for neediness. Well, that's a topic for another blog.

awkward
man hugs

WHEN DID SHAKING HANDS AS A GREETING GO OUT OF FASHION WITH MEN?

IT SEEMS THAT EVERYWHERE YOU GO
THESE DAYS, YOU CAN SPOT GUYS AWKWARDLY HUGGING.

Restaurants, gyms, sporting events, car shows—wherever men gather, they're engaging in these awkward man hugs. Not quite touching. Holding back as if they're touching too much. No longer content with a fist bump, men are now deep into each other's shoulder space, bent forward, heads apart, as they balance precariously, struggling to make some sort of physical connection.

UBIQUITOUS HUGGING

If you watch sports, it's everywhere. Touchdown! Give me a hug. Three-pointer! Body slam. Home run! Grab a dude and lift him in the air. For decades, men have been eager to touch as long as they've scored on the field. And these aren't the awkward, stand-back hugs. Oh, no. The celebrations only start when men are leaping, grabbing, and tightly hugging.

So, when did the sports-hugging morph from special events to everyday awkward man-hug behavior? No one really knows. But awkward man-hugging is definitely here to stay.

GAY HUGS

Now, gay men—they know how to hug. They pull you tight into their personal space. Sometimes, you don't know whether they're being friendly or actually feeling you up. Sometimes, it can be both. But when you get a hug from a gay man, it's warm and welcoming. It feels completely like what it is: an embrace of supportive "great to see you" man-admiration.

SHUT UP AND GIVE ME A HUG

Today, we hug anyone we causally meet at a party. Friends of friends. Relatives you don't even like. And if touching strangers is not your thing—well, something's clearly wrong with you.

Years ago, I had a friend who greeted everyone with an arm held stiffly out to signal for you to step back. He refused to hug. And that never changed. Over the years, friends came and went through his revolving friendship door. He never seemed to really connect for too long. In hindsight, that's not surprising. The signs were always there. Beginning with his unwillingness to embrace anyone.

THE LEARN

So, as I go forth, I will embrace my fellow man, gay and straight, and I'll remember that hugging is a way of letting someone know that I'm open to their friendship. And if only our shoulders touch, I will not judge. Instead, I will awkwardly smile and be grateful. For we all need friends. Even the ones who prefer to stand two feet back as they stiffly bend forward.

weather
or
not...

HERE COMES SUMMER

SOME PEOPLE ARE OBSESSED WITH WEATHER. THUNDERSTORMS, TORNADOES, SLEET, HAIL.

A simple snowstorm becomes a nor'easter. Millions without power. At least that's how reporters ramp up the story. But living in Phoenix, we don't have much weather. It's generally sunny and pleasant most of the year—until it isn't. Then it's still sunny and hot. Did I say hot? I mean really hot.

THAT'S A LOT OF ZEROS

When we first moved to Phoenix, the summer seemed unendurable. That's because the triple-digit temperatures start around May 7th and last until roughly October 7th. I know this because I was desperate to put a time limit on the experience. As the snowbirds flew north, we remained. Air conditioners jacked up. Ice water nearby. Pool in constant use.

And oddly enough, it's during a Phoenix summer that you'll see Phoenicians in sweaters. That's because the restaurants and movie theaters are kept at the temperature of a meat locker. We're all wearing lightweight clothing to stave off the heat outside. So, when we step inside, it's quite an experience. At the supermarket, we run past the dairy aisle. The meat counter isn't much better. And pity the poor soul who gets stuck in frozen foods. You can literally build an igloo in that aisle.

SAND ANYONE?

And then there's monsoon season. It kicks in around June 15th and runs through September 30th—with most of the activity in July and August. The monsoons arrive courtesy of the Gulf of Mexico, bringing rain, wind, and dust storms called haboobs. Haboobs present the most dramatic weather of the season. Huge clouds of dust are swept up from the Arizona desert and engulf the area. News stations catch the beginnings of these haboobs as they start to roll. As you wait for them to arrive, the air is still. Then the skies darken, and a massive gust of wind kicks up. You're overtaken by sand as the visibility drops to zero.

Each year my husband and I talk about leaving Phoenix for the summer. Carving that time out for vacations elsewhere. Many people do. But we two have become hardy desert rats. We stay. And each summer, usually around July 30th, we look at each other and desperately plot an escape before we slowly slip back into the pool.

AH THE SUMMER IN PHOENIX. WE'VE COME TO LOVE IT.

arthritis anyone?

I'VE JUST TAKEN AN ALEVE TO
CALM THE PAIN IN MY LEFT THUMB
THAT AN ORTHOPEDIC SURGEON
PRONOUNCED AS ARTHRITIS.

DAMN HIM!

Okay. It happens. None of us are young forever. My dad had the same problem with his left thumb in his mid-40s. That's when he dropped out of his bowling league. He was an awesome bowler until that left thumb started to ache. And, since he was a lefty … well, that wasn't going to work.

Me—I'm a righty. So, this slow deterioration has come without any physical justification. My left thumb is barely used. I don't hitch hike. And, unlike Jack Horner, I don't stick my thumb in pies. Though, if I did, I'd head over to Rock Springs Café in Black Canyon City, Arizona. Spoiler alert: best pies ever. Come visit Arizona and I'll prove it to you.

SO, WHAT GOOD IS A LEFT THUMB?

I don't use my left thumb to type, as my right thumb handles the spacebar. But I do use it to hold the steering wheel when I drive. Yow, that can hurt. And my left thumb is also the preferred digit for ripping open envelopes. I've tried using my right thumb. It just feels so wrong.

NOT THE WORST THING

I guess this isn't the worst thing that could happen to me. People are diag-nosed every day with life-threatening illnesses. What's one left thumb in the scope of all that suffering? Not much. Besides, it gives me an excuse to stop lifting heavy weights at the gym. Instead, that left thumb might enjoy holding onto something icy cold, like a shake from Culver's or Dairy Queen. Come to think of it, I've heard that icing an ache can bring down swelling. Hmm. Now, there's a perfect solution in search of a problem.

I'VE BEEN DRIVING JEFF'S NEW CAR. A LINCOLN MKC.

And, much to my surprise, the whole thing is push-button. The entire shift mechanism is gone. You have to literally point and touch your way to park, reverse, and drive. Great for keeping your mind agile. Not so great for those of us who are still searching for the stick shift.

CHANGE FOR CHANGES SAKE

Every now and then, we hear about an older person behind the wheel who plows through a crowd. That's usually due to confusion between the gas pedal and the brake. And yet, with the graying of America, cars continue to change. Haven't we learned anything? Fortunately, Ford has modified the once complicated *My Ford Touch*. They've gone back to the manual radio and temperature control system. Thank goodness. Traveling at 75 mph on the highway while trying to figure out how to make those minor changes was a death-defying feat. Common sense has prevailed.

SO, HOW'S THE RIDE?

Amazing. Detroit couldn't have made a better car than Jeff's Lincoln MKC. It's luxurious and comfortable. The seats won't inflame your sciatica. The only real problem with the car is that it's not mine. Okay, we do "share and share alike." But, in the end, the Lincoln is Jeff's to drive. I'm still in a 2009 Honda Fit. Utilitarian. Small. Gas-efficient. And a hell of a ride—if you want to feel every pothole in the road.

breaking news

MAN DISCOVERS PEDICURES

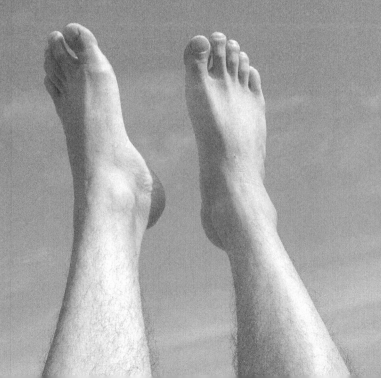

UNLIKE WOMEN WHO LUXURIATE IN PEDICURES, MEN ARE TOUGH.

We manage our own nail care. Bending and straining to clip them until something terrible happens. Like an ingrown toenail. Foot fungus. Fallen arches. And then we rush to the podiatrist. Because that's where men go to manage any issues with their feet. Toenails eventually get clipped—but by a professional with a degree.

NAILS LIKE HOWARD HUGHES

For men who live mostly in colder climates and therefore rarely expose their feet, there's little hope. If you check out those toenails, and I have seen a few, they're in horrible shape. Too long, too dark, too crusty. I won't go on but, trust me, it's disgusting.

I used to live in Michigan, so I know all about hiding your feet. Wearing socks to bed isn't always about staying warm. But for people who live in Phoenix, a hot-weather climate, their toes are on display much of the year. In the summer, everyone wears flip-flops and sandals. We walk around barefoot. We go swimming.

You are the toes that cling to you.

PEDICURES

So, I've finally given in. I've become a regular at my neighborhood nail salon. Every month or so, I sit in a comfortable chair, read the latest issue of *People*, and soak my feet in hot water. I've come to admire the women (they're always women) who have made my toenails look decent. Clipping, scrubbing, buffing—giggling at my discomfort as they remove calluses with what appears to be a cheese grater. And I've been amazed at the transformation.

Finally, my feet are presentable. With regular pedicures, toenails can indeed be your friend.

WHO KNEW?

the
world's
oldestfly

WHERE DID IT COME FROM?

DID YOU EVER NOTICE THAT YOU CAN'T SEEM TO EAT IN A DELI WITHOUT RUNNING INTO A FLY CIRCLING YOUR PASTRAMI SANDWICH?

It drives me nuts. Instead of enjoying my meal, I spend my time guarding the plate, swatting at the air, hoping the filthy creature doesn't land in the coleslaw.

OTHER RESTAURANTS TOO

To be fair, it's not just delicatessens. Many restaurants seem to have the same problem. If there's an open patio, I completely understand. It's just part of the dining experience. Nature will exist where man and even woman chooses to sit. (You can quote me.) But when you're inside and flies are swarming, isn't it the staff's responsibility to eliminate the infestation? Is that really too much to ask?

GREEK WITH A TWIST

A few years ago, Jeff and I ate at a Greek restaurant in Palm Springs. White tablecloths, soft music, and a price point that was amazing. And though the food was delicious, no one on Yelp had bothered to mention the fly situation. With my first taste of eggplant, the flies suddenly appeared. Scarfing down the moussaka, I watched them line up on the windowsill. It was like an Alfred Hitchcock shot from *The Birds*. The flies were soon everywhere. Did we leave? Hell, no. The food was too good. Instead, we hunkered down, gobbling up our meal as we swatted away.

WHAT TO DO?

And so, I wonder, does anyone ever complain about restaurant flies? Is it rude to tell the management you're leaving even after you've just ordered? Are we willing to put up with the flying-critter onslaught if the food exceeds our expectations? And what do you do when they land on your food? Do you continue to eat?

BUCK UP, MAN

I know there are some people who think it's no big deal. I live with one such person. So, I guess I will continue to duck and dodge as I cover my food with one hand while forking it up with the other. But I still think the staff should be trained on how to use a flyswatter. Aim high, swing hard, and splat.

DESSERT ANYONE?

sleeping
beauty

WAKE UP!

I'VE DISCOVERED A NEW TALENT:

I'm able to fall asleep sitting straight up. That's right! Put me in a chair, dim the lights, and I can sleep through the first five minutes of any movie or play. No matter how loud the volume or interested I might be in the subject matter. Regardless of the time of day. I will drift right off.

SLEEPING WELL AT HOME?

Yes, I'm getting enough rest at night, thank you. There's no problem in that department. And I don't have narcolepsy. I'm not falling asleep anytime or anywhere. Just when the setting seems to call for it. Otherwise, I'm perfectly alert. Mostly. Unless the story you're telling me is going on too long, or the jokes aren't funny, or I've heard it all before. In that case, I might suppress a yawn. But only to be polite.

CATNAPS

In general, I'm not a big fan of napping. I never have been. It leaves me feeling groggy. But now I'm beginning to wonder if a catnap—defined as short, light sleep—is required at my age. Does it just come with the territory? If that's true, I can accept it. I just wish I wasn't doing it in public. Especially when I've spent money to be entertained.

JET LAG

I understand being sleepy if you're suffering from jet lag. On our first day in Australia, we met friends at a lovely restaurant for dinner. They invited us back to their home for dessert. The strawberry short cake was amazing. The sugar content alone should have kept me alert for hours. But after I put the cake plate down, I fell asleep. Yes, I did. I was sitting straight up. When I next opened my eyes, the host was staring at me. "Are you okay?" he asked. I was fine. Certainly better rested.

FAMILY HISTORY

My mother used to tell stories about my father, who fell asleep at parties. She thought it was rude. I remember watching television with my dad. He'd often drift off. I'd wait patiently until his eyes opened and then talk to him as if he'd been alert the whole time. "You never told me about that before," I'd say. "So, what happened next?" The look on Dad's face would be priceless. Now, I understand how he felt. Destiny can be harsh!

mahjong
anyone?

FRIENDS INVITED US OVER TO
LEARN HOW TO PLAY MAHJONG. MAHJONG!

The game my mother and her friends played when I was growing up.
I remember those ladies laughing and calling out tiles as I passed through
the kitchen on my way to the refrigerator. I'd hear "two crack, three bam, five
dot," as they rapidly went around the table. They'd smoke cigarettes, sip
refreshments, and talk endlessly. Often their voices would rise in excitement,
rolling into laughter. I never knew what they were talking about. And if I happened to linger too long in the doorway, I was told "keep moving, buster."

MY TURN

So, it was with great interest that I accepted the invitation to join a group of friends learning the game. After all, I thought, rather arrogantly, how hard can it be?

It was hard. Very hard.

And as I struggled to figure out what the hell was going on, I couldn't help but think of my mother. How did she ever carry on a conversation while playing this complicated game? How many rounds did she endure before she no longer needed to concentrate? And why is this game so much harder than poker?

AMERICAN VERSION

It seems that there are two versions of mahjong: the American—which I was learning—and the Chinese—which was being played by a group of men at another table near me. I'm guessing the American version is easier but, being new to it, I still felt it was like learning Hebrew (and that's hard). The other guys kept saying it's like playing gin rummy. I know gin rummy! I get the comparison. But this was beyond gin rummy.

FACEBOOK

And as with all happenings these days, pictures of the event were posted on Facebook. Sure enough, there was a photograph of me concentrating, unable to even look up from the tile rack. What I had assumed would be easy, proved to be quite a challenge.

THE REAL LESSON

Though my mother's been gone nearly thirty years, one afternoon of mahjong brought her right back to me. And as I struggled with the tiles and the rules, I somehow felt deeply connected to her once again. I guess you're never too old to learn new things. Like, learning the game of mahjong and being reminded that your mother was one smart lady.

I MISS YOU, MOM!

and the
password
is...

IN THIS AGE OF THE INTERNET, I HAVE MORE PASSWORDS THEN I CAN POSSIBLY REMEMBER.

Pages and pages of passwords. Many of the new accounts came with the publication of my debut novel, *The Intersect*. Goodreads, Kindle, Apple, and WordPress—to name but a few. The rest are what I refer to as passwords for living. These include Amazon, American Airlines, Southwest, Safeway, Netflix, and countless hotel chains and travel sites. The list has exploded. It seems you can't do anything today without firing up the Internet and creating a new password.

MIX IT UP

I've taken the advice of the tech industry and changed it up when creating my passwords. It makes sense that no two accounts should ever have the same password. If they hack into your bank, you certainly don't want them to have access to your electronic medical record. Though if they hack into your bank account, who really cares if they know I was at the doctor twice in April due to a nagging case of bronchitis? I'd prefer they just not touch my money, such as it is. Cough be damned.

CREATING A PASSWORD

We've been told to avoid names or birth dates and to combine numbers and letters along with symbols ($#&!) to the password string. The days of using a simple "123456" are over. Phrases aren't a bad idea, but then, you have to be able to remember them. Any chance of a simple, easy-to-remember password has been shot to hell.

IGNORANCE IS NO EXCUSE

There are fee-based password management services ready to coordinate all this for you. Of course, they require that you create a *master password*. That made me laugh! I know I should have more confidence, but with so many places being hacked, why wouldn't a company that secures passwords be a prime target itself?

CREATIVITY

So, I continue to add passwords to my handwritten sheets, and in an odd way, it's become an exercise in creativity. When I look through my passwords, it's like scanning a twisted version of my coded life. So, let those thieves try to figure out my passwords. I dare them. Did I add a $ sign or a % sign? Two numbers or twenty? I'll never tell.

summer movies

OR HOW TO SURVIVE PHOENIX IN JULY

EVERYONE KNOWS PHOENIX IS HOT IN THE SUMMER.

That's when most Phoenicians plan their vacations. But for those who stay in town and want to leave the house in the afternoon, the choices are limited. There's the air-conditioned restaurant, a trip to the supermarket, or a walk through a shopping mall. And, yes, there's the movie theater.

SENIOR DISCOUNT

I admit it. I love the matinee show as much as I love my senior discount. I know. It's not a huge saving. But to me, it's a big deal. For years I stayed away from the movie theater because it was so darn expensive. Call it price sensitivity or consumer activism; either way, I opted instead for Netflix. But watching a movie at home pales to the experience in a darkened theater. Who wants to sit in their living room when you can view a movie on a large screen with those great theater acoustics?

DINE-IN OPTION

Unlike my friends, I dislike the dine-in option when I go to the movies. I like to see my food when I eat. I'm visual that way. I want to make sure everything looks okay before I put it in my mouth. In the dark, that becomes a challenge. Besides, I'm a man of limited focus. I can either eat or enjoy the movie. Not both. And, based on the amount of stain remover used in our house, I'm also a messy eater. And that's even when I can see what I'm doing.

FORTUNES ARE BUILT ON MEAGER SAVINGS

I'm often astonished by those patrons who buy out the concession stands. You've seen them as they struggle with their king-size popcorn, large drinks, and nacho chips with queso. Balancing all that food on their lap as they munch away. Forget all the calories they're consuming; the cost of those snacks dwarfs the movie's ticket price. I often think those people could benefit from an intervention by a good money manager. Where's Charles Schwab when you need him? But, to be truthful, I hate sitting in a darkened theater listening to other people slurping their drinks or munching on popcorn. When I'm watching a movie, I want to be engrossed in the film. Not what the person next to me is eating.

CRABBY OLD FART?

Yes, I know. That's how it sounds. And perhaps that's who I am these days. But I think movie theaters are for being transported to another world, not stuffing your face. There. I said it! Go eat lunch somewhere else. And while I'm at it, stop all that gosh-darn coughing and sneezing. If you're sick, stay home. I'm trying to watch the movie!

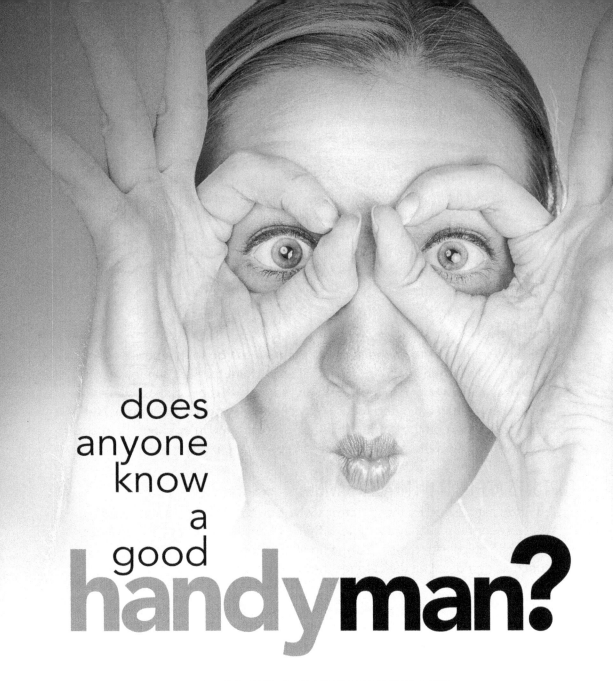

does anyone know a good **handyman?**

GEE, IT'S AWFULLY HARD TO FIND A HANDYMAN THESE DAYS.

Someone affordable who can provide electrical, carpentry, and plumbing services. I've searched online. Asked neighbors and friends. No one seems to have a recommendation. How can that be? Meanwhile, doctors, lawyers, and financial planners seem to be everywhere. Always advertising their services. You can hardly turn around without tripping over them.

AMERICAN AIRLINES

On a recent trip to San Francisco, the in-flight magazine profiled *The Top Doctors in America*. I'd never considered flying to Nashville to meet an orthopedic surgeon. Or to Los Angeles for a plastic surgery consultation. Or to Baltimore to visit an Ob/Gyn (but then in my case that would just be silly). Pages and pages of physicians reaching out across the country. Each one guaranteed to be the best in his or her field.

DUI?

And relaxing in front of the television watching Judge Judy (I'm a sucker for a woman who likes to say "kerfuffle"), the commercials begin for lawyers. Lots of catchy tunes. One gentleman (clearly over sixty) rides a motorcycle without a helmet and sports an extremely tight T-shirt displaying a buff physique (I'm just saying). Another pair is a husband-and-wife team. They seem happily married (but who can really tell?), smiling for the camera. Then, there's this huge office staff, one after another claiming to represent the best law firm. Which explains why, if you call the office, you're guaranteed to never speak to either of the actual lawyers they're promoting. That seems like an odd marketing strategy.

I TAKE MY STEAK MEDIUM RARE

Financial planners are constantly inviting me to join them for fancy dinners at high-end restaurants. I've yet to accept, but I've been tempted. I love Morton's and Ruth's Chris, but financial planners…not so much. And still, I think it might be my duty to explore those offers. I hate to think of all that great food going to waste.

BUT NO HANDYMAN

So where are the handymen? (Handywomen? Handypersons?) Someone to hang a light fixture, fix a closet door, paint a back fence, or repair a garbage disposal. They've gone the way of the dinosaur. Or they've specialized and become professional electricians, carpenters, and plumbers. Now those firms seem to be everywhere, too. Advertising on TV right next to the doctors, lawyers, and the financial planners. But they aren't offering fancy steak dinners. I wish they were. Gosh, I love steak!

saving
it for good

YEARS AGO, A WISE FAMILY FRIEND SHARED WITH ME THE PHRASE "SAVING IT FOR GOOD."

I wasn't quite sure what she meant, but I knew right away, from the tone of her voice and facial expression, that saving it for good was not a great idea.

LIFE IS SHORT

Perhaps there are clothes hanging in the closet that you've never worn. Or unplanned vacations that you hope to take one day. Or friends you'd like to visit—but have yet to find the right time. Then you know all about saving it for good. It means waiting for that perfect moment to savor life's pleasures.

CONTROL IS AN ILLUSION

It's often said that *life is what happens as we're busy making other plans.* John Lennon sang about it in *Beautiful Boy.* And so, my wise family friend was probably trying to convey to me that it's a mistake to save it for good. We truly only have this moment. Not yesterday. And there are no promises of tomorrow.

TAKE IT TO HEART

I've tried to be mindful of that counsel, though I often fall short. I tend to save it for good, often putting things off. Not ordering a chocolate malted because to do so would require some achievement to celebrate. It's like being an inverted optimist: never quite satisfied with today, while hoping tomorrow will bring something wonderful. Which, on reflection, seems like a great way to miss out on your life.

is your
refrigerator
a mess?

I WISH MY REFRIGERATOR WERE BRAND SPANKING NEW.

Perfectly clean with all my favorite foods lined up on shelves that sparkled. Labels facing front so that you could read them. Tupperware neatly stacked. No crumbs or wet spots anywhere.

A LITTLE OCD?

Yes, I'm neat. But not a neat freak. I don't mind if a drawer is messy—as long as it's closed. The bedroom closet may need some straightening up, but not every day. And frankly, I'm okay with the state of our garage. Of course, it's easy to pass through there quickly. Really—who lingers in a garage? But the refrigerator? That feels different. Maybe it's because I spend so much time looking inside it.

VOILÀ!

Think of how a trained chef dresses a plate. It's more than just the food— it's about eye appeal. How the colors balance. How the shapes contrast. It's lending an artistic eye so that everything presents in an appetizing way to heighten the experience.

OLDER MODELS

The fact is, older homes, like mine, come with older refrigerators. I've tried taking apart the shelves in our refrigerator and washing out every nook and cranny. I've even tried ordering new shelves and drawers. But the model is so old, everything is out of stock. *Discontinued* can be such an ugly word.

ONE DAY

If dreams come true, one day I will look inside our refrigerator and be overwhelmed by its sparkling brilliance. All my favorite foods will be lined up in beautifully coordinated containers. A loving voice will say—*Brad, what would you like to eat? The fruit bin is empty, but we have chocolate cake, rice pudding, and ice cream.*

death

&new
orleans

A FEW WEEKS AGO, I WAS IN NEW ORLEANS TO CELEBRATE A FRIEND'S BIRTHDAY.

The city seemed to be full of funereal fun. Seriously. The tourist shops were stocked with voodoo dolls, death masks, and skeletons. Everywhere you turned there were signs of decay. Above-ground mausoleums—crumbling and creepy. And the ghost tours! It seemed as if some poor soul has died a violent death on every corner in New Orleans. I guess that's what happens when a city is situated below sea level. People are macabre.

1986?

But it wasn't until I separated from my traveling companions for a few hours that I began to remember. New Orleans was where I'd initially vacationed with Richard, my first partner, some thirty-five years earlier. He was a second-year ophthalmology resident at Henry Ford Hospital in Detroit at the time. A few years later, he graduated from his residency, became board certified, and landed his first job. Within weeks, however, he became ill. He died of AIDS in July 1989. He was only thirty-three years old.

STARTLED BY THE RECALL

As I walked around the gift shops, I thought about Richard. The pink and purple masks we'd bought that hung on the wall of our first apartment. Our breakfast at Brennan's, when we first ate Bananas Foster. Richard's delight in Cafe Du Monde and the deep-fried beignets covered in confectionary sugar. We were together again as I examined the handicrafts and listened to the live music in Jackson Square.

TRAGEDY

When someone you love dies, the pain seems unbearable. Especially when the cause is as silly as a virus. I remember that pain. And so, as I walked around Jackson Square, listening to the musicians and watching the jugglers, I refocused on the present. After all, New Orleans has made a pretty penny hyping the past to tourists. I didn't need to be reminded that death can be tragic, uninvited, and often heartbreaking. I already knew.

smartphone etiquette

STOP LOOKING AT YOUR DAMN PHONE

THE OTHER NIGHT, I WAS AT DINNER WITH FRIENDS.

Within minutes of being seated, we were all looking down at our smart-phones—Googling, Facebooking, and God only knows what else. To be fair, our phones have become critical to supporting our conversations. It seems none of us can remember the relevant information we used to have at our fingertips. Who was in the movie I saw last night? (Melissa McCarthy) What is that politician's last name? (Buttigieg) Is that person alive or dead? (Pick any Hollywood star) And where are they buried? (James Dean is in Indiana) What's the capital of India? (New Delhi) And where's the Taj Mahal located? (Agra)

As I glanced about the table, I wondered if we were truly struggling with our memories or merely suffering from Nomophobia?

NOMO WHAT?

Nomophobia: The fear of being without your mobile phone (*"no mobile phone"*—shortened to Nomo). Is this the new frontier of addiction? It's so sad. Time lost with loved ones because our attention has wandered to the technology in our hand.

MILLENNIALS

I've heard it said that the generation raised with smartphones is struggling with the development of their social skills. To be honest, it hasn't done much for people my age, either. All of us now text. It's so much easier than having a "real" conversation. And Facebook gives us the false sense that we're in *touch* even though you can't actually *touch* anyone. Facebook *friends* create the illusion that we're loved or important or part of something bigger than ourselves. In reality, we're just sitting alone—observing other people's lives.

I guess that's better than nothing.

I'VE FALLEN INTO THE TRAP AND I CAN'T CLIMB OUT

Those of us who aspire to be successful writers are told to "expand our reach." People need to know who we are in order to trust that they might enjoy our work. I doubt Hemingway or Fitzgerald had an ongoing relationship with their public—but then, I'm no Ernest or F. Scott. Still, can you imagine those two literary giants texting? Now, Dorothy Parker—she'd have excelled at tweeting in 280 characters. Still, being witty 24/7 is a challenge for any modern author. Best to say nothing at all. At least, then you can retain some semblance of quiet intelligence.

ENGAGE

So, the next time you go to dinner, avoid taking out your smartphone. Unless, of course, you need to look something up, like the meaning of "steak poivre." Or you want to show the most recent photos of the family. Or you simply must answer that annoying ring tone. And as you check your smartphone, know that your friends will be rolling their eyes as they post about your Nomophobia on their Facebook page.

why
is a
poodle
in
the
bath
room
?

WHEN I GREW UP IN NEW YORK CITY IN THE 1960S, A POODLE LIVED IN OUR BATHROOM.

Pink, with black eyes and a white bow permanently sewn to its head, he sat atop the back of the toilet tank, beady eyes watching our family during the most intimate of moments. By now you've probably guessed that the crocheted body with four tiny legs and a bouncy tail concealed the extra roll of toilet tissue.

IS THIS ONLY FOR COMPANY?

When you live in a two-bedroom, one-bath apartment like ours was then, there seems to be a decorating dilemma. The single bathroom serves both family and guests. And so, along with the poodle cozy, there were decorative hand towels that we didn't touch. And now that I think about it, I never did see that poodle lying atop the tank disemboweled. Our stuffed poodle was a permanent fixture. The order of the day: Reach under the sink if you need to replace the roll.

BAD TOILET TRAINING?

Years later, the lessons learned in my childhood are hard to shake. And though we don't have a poodle cozy for the extra roll of toilet tissue, I remain unwilling to use our decorative hand towels. Why should I have this reaction in my own home? It must be the result of my early, well, toilet training.

COZY? NOT

The rule in our house is that when we expect guests, all rolls of toilet tissue are refreshed in advance. We don't want guests to rummage through the cabinets in search of fulfillment. God forbid. Which makes me wonder if a whimsical poodle cozy might be the perfect addition to our bathroom décor. It would certainly match our Dalmatian toilet brush holder.

ever
walk
into
your
beloved?

ARE YOU CLUMSY? *OR* IS IT SOMETHING ELSE?

IT'S ODD, BUT FOR SOME REASON OUR HOUSE DOESN'T SEEM TO BE BIG ENOUGH.

Oh, there's plenty of square footage. Certainly, enough for two men and a dog to navigate. And yet, we seem to be constantly bumping into each other. I can't quite figure it out.

POINTS OF CONTACT

The foot traffic is swiftest in the hallway. Living in the Sonoran Desert, we drink a lot of water. It's not unusual for us to nearly knock each other down crossing back and forth to the bathroom. But our most popular rendezvous is in front of the refrigerator. Here is where we have real fender-benders. Squeezing by, accusing the other of being in the wrong place at the wrong time. Meanwhile, our dog hovers nearby, standing guard at his bowl, believing we're engaged in a struggle over who will win the great honor of feeding him (again, since moments ago).

NAVIGATING BLIND CORNERS

There's nothing worse than being frightened by the sudden appearance of the only other person in the house. It often seems that Jeff has materialized right out of thin air. After I jump, he'll say indignantly, "I live here, too!" Perhaps, because we both work out of the same space, we've become oblivious to the other. Talk about focus and intense powers of concentration! I'm beginning to think about attaching a bell to him.

FOOTSTEPS ON THE PATH

Years ago, a friend said he'd seen us from a distance in the supermarket and that we were standing very close together. If that's true, perhaps that's why we keep bumping into each other. I guess if you walk through life together, it's expected that sometimes your foot lands in the same spot. Or maybe we're just clumsy. I wonder if that can be it?

if the sky is up

...WHY AM I LOOKING DOWN?

I HATE TO ADMIT IT, BUT I SPEND A LOT OF TIME LOOKING DOWN.

Ever since I was a kid, my eyes have been cast toward the pavement. Through the years, I've wondered whether this is a concern for safety, not wanting to trip, or a reflection of my innate personality. Am I making too much of this? If so, it certainly wouldn't be the first time.

AVOIDING POTHOLES?

It isn't that I'm afraid of falling. My balance is okay. Of course, there are nights when I stumble along in the dark to you-know-where. When I first step out of bed, my feet are stiff—curled tightly—like claws. Eventually, the muscles relax. I look like a parrot walking along, shifting left to right. Fortunately, no one can see me. Except the dog. Move, and he's wide awake hoping it's time for a moonlight walk.

IT'S NOT ABOUT SHOES

I'm not looking down because I'm fascinated with shoes. I could care less. Though in Phoenix, flip-flops almost pass for formal wear. And then there's the occasional lady in high, spiky heels. It's amazing to watch her balance on stilts. It's like watching a circus act without a net.

NEW YORK CITY KID

I think the real reason I look down is based on where I was raised. In New York City, you just don't make eye contact with strangers. Not unless you need something. Otherwise, you're only asking for trouble. No one wants to be on the end of *Hey man, what are you looking at?!* Best to keep your gaze downward, to avoid the dangerous elements populating the world. Little boys have been beaten up for much less.

GLASS HALF-EMPTY

I seem to be the cautious type. I've stepped in enough dog poop to know that it can't be avoided by admiring the birds in the trees. But secretly, I'd like to do just that. To walk boldly forward, head held high, enjoying a beautiful sunset. Unconcerned about the next step. Eyes upward, searching the sky. It's still possible, I guess. Unlikely, but still possible.

why
is the medicine cabinet in the kitchen?

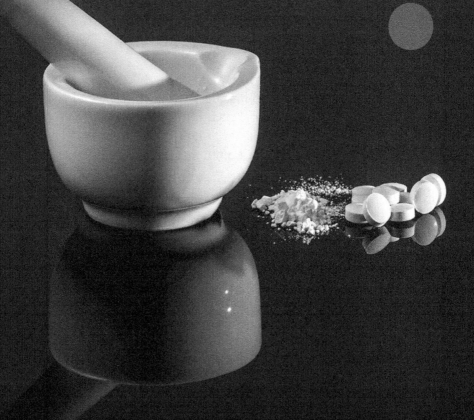

THE OTHER DAY, I WENT TO A KITCHEN DRAWER FOR HEARTBURN MEDICATION.

Food can generate heartburn, so it makes sense to store a roll of Tums nearby instead of having to walk all the way to the master bath.

BUT THE DRAWER IS FULL

At first, I couldn't find the Tums. That's because the drawer was loaded with over-the-counter medications. From Gas-X to Tagamet to Advil. From Tylenol to Aleve to Mucinex. Alka-Seltzer Cold and Flu, Gaviscon, Nexium, and chewable vitamin C. The drawer was brimming with health remedies. It made me wonder. Are we really this ill?

MEDICINE CABINET

We don't have a medicine cabinet in our house. Instead, we have drawers in the bathroom that provide ample space for everything we might need. Upon recent inspection, we seem to need a lot. How many first-aid creams are required to heal a cut? Does Airborne protect you when you fly? Does magnesium really support a healthy immune system? We live in a pill-popping society. Perhaps with a healthier diet, we could skip the Pepto-Bismol and Dulcolax altogether.

EXPIRATION

Once a year, I think about going through all these meds to check expiration dates. But I don't. Frankly, it seems too overwhelming. Instead, I commit to checking the labels before using the actual product. Frankly, I think it's a waste of time to do that with cough syrup. Robitussin is so disgusting—going bad can only improve the taste.

AGING OR CONVENIENCE?

So, when did the medicine cabinet move to the kitchen? Is it a function of aging or simply convenience? Are you experiencing the same phenomenon in your home? If so, how many drawers are you using? And if your drawers are stuffed like mine, is it really fair, when people ask, to tell them, "I feel great!"

ten✓tips
for a happy life

YEARS AGO, I LEARNED AN IMPORTANT LESSON WHEN SOMEONE I LOVED WAS DYING.

If you can throw money at a problem and fix it, then it really isn't a problem. Of course, that philosophy requires access to cash. Line up a roof repair, a new hot water tank, and a balloon mortgage, and that wisdom is hard to remember. And yet, I'd bet you'd agree that we all give too much emotional weight to minor irritations. They're annoying, yes. But not permanent.

DO AS I SAY, NOT AS I DO

So today, I thought I'd share my coping strategies when faced with life's little bugaboos. The things that drive me crazy and the solutions that I've devised to let go of the negative energy. I'll just cover a few for your consideration. They're simple and don't require much explanation. If they make you smile…then I've done my job.

THE GOLDEN TEN

1 WHEN YOU DON'T HAVE TIME
TO CLEAN THE HOUSE—
DIM THE LIGHTS

*Everything looks better
in the dark.*

2 IF YOU HEAR A RATTLING IN THE
CAR WHILE YOU'RE DRIVING—TURN
UP THE VOLUME ON THE RADIO.

*That pen rolling around in the glove
compartment can wait until you've
come to a full stop.*

3 EVERYTHING TODAY IS MADE WITH
AN EMBEDDED COMPUTER CHIP.

*Before you call India to fix a problem—
reboot by shutting down, unplugging,
and counting to thirty before plugging
back in and trying again.*

4 BROWNIES, ICE CREAM, AND
CHOCOLATE TOPPING ARE THE
FASTEST CURE FOR THE BLUES

*This also works well if you're
bored or lonely.*

5 ALL OF THE GROCERY CARTS AT
WALMART HAVE AT LEAST
ONE BROKEN WHEEL.

*That's the price you must pay
for deep discounts.*

6 NO MATTER HOW YOUR DOG
STARES INTO YOUR EYES, HE ISN'T
DESPERATELY IN LOVE WITH YOU.

*He probably wants to eat, poop,
or play. Maybe all three.*

7 LOVE IS NOT A GIVEN.

*Act loving—and you're bound to get
some loving back. Behave badly—and
watch your world turn upside down.*

8 FEAR IS THERE TO WARN US.

*But then, it likes to play with your head.
Face your fears and you might
surprise yourself.*

9 AGE IS ALL IN YOUR MIND.

*Until you ache. Then it's in your
thumb, toe, and elbow.*

10 HAPPINESS REQUIRES THAT
YOU FOCUS ON SOMETHING
OTHER THAN YOURSELF.

*True happiness is found
in helping others.*

TAKE WHAT YOU WANT . . . PITCH THE REST

I hope these little truths resonate with you. They're beliefs I hold dear, though I haven't always managed to live by them. It's a funny thing about being human: The next drama always seems to be lurking just around the corner, waiting for us to pick up the script and read our lines. Every now and then, it helps to break the habit. To refuse to play the part. I wish I'd done that more often in my life. I guess there's still time to learn.

why is the **television** so darn loud?

SOMETHING'S GOING ON IN OUR HOUSE. SOMETHING INEXPLICABLE.

The volume on the television is extremely loud. Until it isn't. And then, you have to struggle to understand the words spoken by the actors.

WHAT?

If you read my blog—and, by the way, thank you for doing so—you know I'm deaf in my left ear. One hundred percent deaf since I was two years old. A case of pneumonia that killed the nerve. Nonetheless, I'm keenly aware of the volume on the television. And if in doubt, I live with someone who can hear perfectly. At least that's what my right ear hears him say, after I repeat myself because he appears not to be listening.

COMMERCE IN ACTION

I realize that when commercials are playing the volume is always louder. That's so you can hear the commercial whether you're in the bathroom or standing in front of an open refrigerator (my two favorite spots during commercial breaks).

Okay, I get it.

But what about when you're streaming Amazon or Netflix? There are no commercials. And still, the music to "Mr. Selfridge" is blaring. If I lower the volume, I can barely make out what anyone is saying. Are they mumbling? Is it their British accent? (Yes, I know, Jeremy Piven is American.) Or have the actors in the series attended the *Marlon Brando School of Mumbling?*

THE MERM

This all brings Ethel Merman to mind. She was legendary. She never needed a mic. She could be heard in every corner of any theater. And with perfect diction. Check her out singing a song from *Annie Get Your Gun*. Yes, she's loud. Brooklyn accent and all. But I guarantee you'll understand every word.

are you too old to change?

to change

WHY YOU SHOULD
RECONSIDER

ONE WAY

YEARS AGO,

my mother rebuffed the news of my coming out by explaining that she couldn't deal with it. Her exact words. "I'm too old to change."

BUT SHE WAS ONLY 55!

It rarely happens in life that you achieve a moment of perfect clarity. But at that moment it was like a lightning bolt coming out of the blue. I made a silent vow right then to open myself up to the possibilities of life. I'd do my best to never be *too old to change*.

CHANGE IS HARD

And it has been a challenge. Over the years, I've moved from city to city. Changed jobs. My career in healthcare has had its ups and downs. Mostly ups, until our last move to Phoenix. By then, I'd landed in the wrong organization. It was a poor cultural fit. The right title and money, but the wrong organization. It took courage to make another choice. The thing about change is, sometimes we need to be careful about what we wish for, and to know when it makes sense to say, "No, thank you" and to move on.

CAREER AS A WRITER

I'm grateful for many things in my life, but none more than that one insight from Mom. She suffered a lot of emotional pain by living with that *too old to change* mantra. And though it's a wonderful thing to hear affirmations from those we love, sometimes it's their judgments and limitations that force us to become our better selves. My mother offered that gift, so I'll be forever grateful to her. By *learning to change*, my life has turned out to be a lot better than I ever expected.

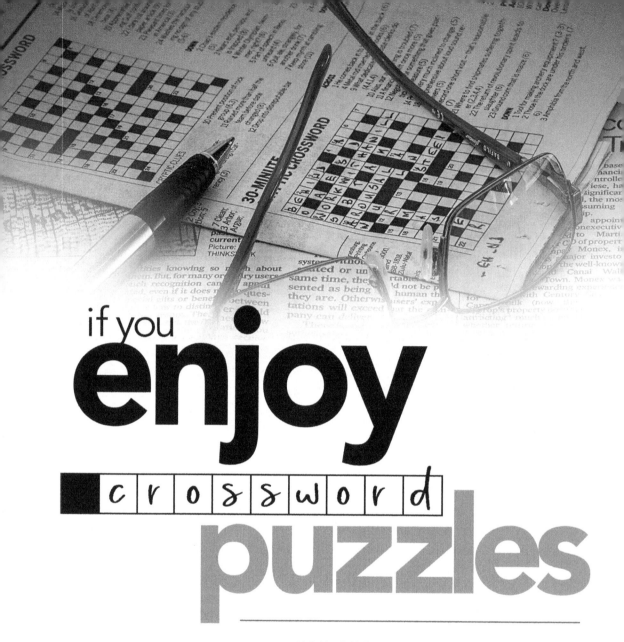

if you enjoy

c r o s s w o r d

puzzles

... YOU SHOULD WRITE A NOVEL

I'VE BEEN WORKING DILIGENTLY ON A THIRD NOVEL, WITH THE GOAL OF PUBLICATION IN LATE 2020.

That would add up to two years to generate my fourth book. Or, two-thirds the time it took for me to finish my debut novel, *The Intersect*. It's a relief to think I might have learned a few things along the way. So, in the spirit of being open, let me share a few insights.

THE LEARN

1 - In the words of Dorothy Parker, "Writing is the art of applying the ass to the seat." In following her advice, I've discovered my hip flexors, sacroiliac, and glute muscles. Yow!

2 - Writing and speaking can be done in the same voice but not at the same time. Too much talking, and I can't write. And after hours of writing, I'm unable to utter an intelligent sentence.

3 - If I don't shed a tear when I'm working on an emotional scene, there's something wrong. This should not be confused with the tears that I shed when I can't get a scene right.

4 - If you respect your characters, they speak on their own. Dialogue is easy! If you try to control them, they rebel and make you the fool.

5 - You need to believe in yourself as a writer before anyone else will. Then, you need to hire a terrific editor to teach you all that you're doing wrong.

6 - Eating is a major component of the creative process. Any food will do. But try to stay away from items purchased at Costco. Large quantities can be polished off in short order.

7 - If you love crossword puzzles, you'd love writing a novel. Words connect scenes. Themes carry through. And everything that you put down on paper can have an alternate meaning.

8 - It's truly satisfying when someone enjoys your work and takes the trouble to write or email you a note. It's even better when they go to Amazon.com and post a review.

9 - The arc of creation matches the bell curve. At the start, there's excitement as the story unfolds. At its peak, you're certain it's all working beautifully. On publication, you're sure you've screwed the whole thing up.

10 - There's a seed of truth about the author's life in every novel. Just a seed. If it were all true, it would be called a memoir!

LAST THOUGHT

I'm grateful to those who continue to read my blog. It's my attempt to stay connected and to share a bit of myself. Thank you for continuing to welcome me into your life. And if you're not yet receiving my blog, it's never too late to sign up at: **www.bradgraber.com**

the **holiday** season is here

_____

YEAH!

_____

THE HOLIDAYS ARE HERE AGAIN, AND THERE'S EXCITEMENT IN THE AIR.

Lots of parties, Burl Ives is singing "Frosty the Snowman" and the morning temperatures in Phoenix are hovering in the fifties. For those experiencing snow and ice, that doesn't sound too bad. But for those of us who've managed through months of triple digits, fifty degrees is awfully cold. We've pulled out our sweaters with the full knowledge that it's now or never.

HANUKAH ANYONE?

Although I grew up in New York City, I really don't recall a lot of buzz about Hanukah. It always seemed to be the poor stepsister to Christmas. The gorgeous, enormous tree in Rockefeller Center. The Radio City Music Hall Rockettes high-kicking in their Santa suits—though, of course, Santa wears pants, not tights and high heels. There was no big hoop-de-doo around spinning the dreidel—though everyone loves potato pancakes and Hanukah gelt: those coin-shaped chocolates covered in gold foil.

YES, CHRISTMAS IS FOR EVERYONE

No matter your religion, cultural affiliation, or whether you even believe in God, Christmas is really a magical time. Heck, if Ebenezer Scrooge can find the true meaning of Christmas, there's hope for us all. So, to everyone reading this today, I wish you the best of the holiday season. Chestnuts roasting on an open fire. Sleigh bells ringing. The "Hallelujah Chorus." And to my Jewish friends and family, remember that it was Irving Berlin who wrote "White Christmas." Hey, that holiday spirit is just contagious.

it's a
new year!

IT'S THE START OF ANOTHER YEAR,
AND I AM FEELING TREMENDOUSLY ENERGIZED.

For those who know me well, this seems an odd turn of events. Typically, I'm miserable this time of year. Not only because there is another Brad birthday looming— and really, who wants to be another year older?—but because the notion of the New Year requires us to focus on making some monumental improvement in our lives.

THAT JUST PUTS TOO MUCH PRESSURE ON THE MONTH OF JANUARY.

Especially when you can choose any time of the year to make improvements. Perhaps, every day. Okay—that's too much for anyone. But you get my drift.

SO WHY WOULD I BE HAPPY?

I've never been one to have New Year's resolutions. I don't operate that way. Instead, as issues arise, I like to make adjustments to my life. It may take me a while to get there, but eventually, I figure out what to do. If you don't believe me, you can just check with any of my former therapists. (Yes, there have been more than one.) I'm certain they'd all give me an A-plus. I was especially good at *timely payment.*

THE AUTHOR'S JOURNEY

But I think the real motivator for me in recent years has been the insurmountable odds of ever becoming a successful author—and in an odd way that's freeing. If it happens, it happens. But it's so darn unlikely that everyone kind of feels sorry for you. I like that. I like that a lot. Sympathy can be immensely gratifying. And I also love a good challenge. Because when you're at the bottom, the only way forward is up. And since everything is still new, it's very exciting.

THE TRICK

When you're just starting out as a writer, no one really knows you, so things can only get better. Oh my God! That must be the silver lining…the world through rose-colored glasses…imagining a brighter future! So, this year, no fad diets, no crazy gym stunts, and no wishing for what "could have been." I'm simply going to be content with what is and feel grateful for the friendship and support of my friends and readers. Who could ask for a better start to a New Year?

fast food for a slow eater?

IT'S TRUE. I EAT FAST FOOD EVERY NOW AND THEN.

You know the places: sticky tables, dirty bathrooms, lots of screaming kids. It happens mostly on road trips. And though I'm a picky eater, I have to admit the food is pretty good. I guess there's no accounting for taste. (I couldn't resist that little play on words. Forgive me.)

WHAT'S THE DEAL WITH THE SODA?

Most fast-food joints offer patrons free refills, even when sodas are sold in a small, medium, or large size. So why would anyone buy a large drink when they can refill the cheaper size? I get how it works with the drive-through. But for the eat-in crowd? Perhaps it has something to do with the labor of walking over to the soda dispenser for another refill. Or maybe folks just prefer the larger cup. I'm sure they've done market research on this, but frankly, it has me stumped.

SAY IT'S NOT TRUE

Now, I don't particularly like soda. A small cola is more than enough for me. To be honest, the carbonation gives me heartburn. Or maybe it's the burger and fries. Thank goodness they don't offer free refills on the fries. Especially at McDonald's. Those fries are damn good. But you must eat them quickly. If you allow them to cool, they assume a rubbery consistency. But when they're piping hot, stand back. It's french fry time!

FRIED CHICKEN...THE GUILTY PLEASURE

And talking about good, who could resist a bucket of southern fried chicken? Friends rave about Church's. When I was a kid, fried chicken was the only thing I'd eat at a restaurant. Back then, it was a staple. But in today's health-conscious world, it's nearly impossible to find fried chicken on a menu. When my family lived in California, there was a Kentucky Fried Chicken in downtown Mill Valley. That particular KFC, as I recall, was busted twice for drugs. I'm certain that wasn't part of Colonel Sander's plan, but with recreational marijuana now approved in California, I can't imagine a better point of distribution.

CULVER'S

And how could I write a blog about fast food without mentioning Culver's? If you haven't been there, come to Phoenix and I'll take you. My treat! Bring the whole family. That's because Culver's has the best fast food, not to mention the most wonderful frozen custard in the universe. Unfortunately, they post the calories on the big board behind the cash registers. They should take that down. It ruins the experience. Is it worth eating frozen custard when it's only seventy-five degrees out? Hit triple digits—and we don't care about calories. Heck, we're in survival mode then. And nothing makes a tastier survival treat than Culver's frozen custard. I personally recommend the chocolate malted. Just saying.

late**night**

buying $pree...

I WAS UP THE OTHER NIGHT, UNABLE TO SLEEP.

It happens. Not often, but enough to know that late-night television is jammed with thirty-minute infomercials. Celebrity promos encouraging us to purchase all sorts of products. From Cindy Crawford's Meaningful Beauty (let's just agree the woman is gorgeous, and even after three decades she looks practically the same) to Leandro Carvalho's (I have no idea who he is but he's very enthusiastic) Brazilian Butt Lift, which finally answers that burning

STAIR STEPPER

In 1990, before anyone ever heard the name Kardashian, I purchased a mini-stair-stepper promoted by Bruce Jenner (this was before he switched genders). It looked like a wonderful piece of exercise equipment and, sure enough, I stepped my way along with the nightly news for all of three weeks until it started to leak grease all over my carpet. By then, the little stepper was making a high-pitched, whining noise. It sounded like I was choking a cat. I wrote Bruce an angry letter complaining about the poorly built stepper. I asked how an Olympian could ever promote such a piece of junk. Needless to say, he never wrote back. As I learned later, his wife Kris had negotiated the deal. So, in a way, I was an early adopter of the Kardashian business model. No comment.

AND I SHOULD HAVE LEARNED MY LESSON...BUT I DIDN'T

Next, I fell victim to a very sincere Hugh Downs. This was well after his retirement from the prime-time news magazine *20/20*. He was promoting a two-volume edition of alternative medical treatments. The pitch: cures the pharmaceutical companies don't want you to know. As a healthcare administrator and part-time hypochondriac, I couldn't resist. At 2:00 a.m., I placed my order. When the books arrived, they were essentially bundled scientific research papers.

LET'S SHOP

Clearly, our defenses are down when we can't sleep. Lately, I've found myself mesmerized by the ads promoting prostate health (it's my age), the perfect cup of coffee (single serving vs. full pot), and age spots (I don't have them, but that doesn't seem to stop me from being concerned). I miss the days of *Bowflex* and Richard Simmons when the infomercials were awe-inspiring and entertaining. And though I love Valerie Bertinelli, I'm not sure that listening to her marvel at how manageable her hair has become with *WEN* is quite up to the same standard. But still, I sit and watch, all the while wondering if infomercials will someday be the sole source of information for our buying decisions. It could happen. Just consult George Orwell or Ray Bradbury. Better yet, watch YouTube.

the game of life:

WHAT'S YOUR SCORE?

THERE'S BEEN A STRANGE TURN IN
OUR LOCAL NEWSPAPER, THE *ARIZONA REPUBLIC.*

Let me explain. They've recently relocated the obituaries to the back of the sports section. Yes, that's right. You can now check game scores while you peruse the passing of your neighbors. How convenient!

SMILE FOR THE CAMERA

The redesign of the obits started weeks ago. First, they enlarged the photographs. I get it. You want your friends and neighbors to actually see the face of your departed loved one. But most of the photographs aren't professionally shot. The enhanced size looks grainy. And as we older folks know, it's hard to capture a flattering photograph, even on our best day. We need proper lighting, some posing, and a bit of photo shopping. Otherwise, Aunt Gertie might look as if she was caught by surprise. Uncle Milton, in the middle of chewing. So why, for heaven's sake (I had to throw that in), make these rag-tag photographs even larger?

THE WHOLE THING HAS GOT ME THINKING (UH OH)

By placing the obits in the sports section, is the *Arizona Republic* confirming that *life is but a game and there are winners and losers?* Is your age at the time of death the ultimate score? If you've reached eighty, ninety, or even one hundred—have you officially won, thus making death the *eternal booby prize?* Or, are the winners determined by the length of the obituary and the scads of relatives who adored them (though God knows they never came to visit)? Does your obit dominate the page, attracting the most attention? And if you're dead, does any of this truly matter?

I GUESS WINNER IS A RELATIVE TERM

Few obits seem to provide the most interesting *highlights* from a life well-lived. I'm not referring to the marriages or the children or even the jobs held. Those are facts. Our lives are shaped by our challenges, hardships, and lessons learned. If you were a parent, what tips can you pass on about raising children? If you were a caretaker for an elderly parent, how did you sustain your enthusiasm? If you succeeded in business, what secrets did you learn about working with people? Just imagine what a terrific read that might be. To capture a snapshot of the living, breathing, thinking human being—and not just vital statistics.

MY *PARTING* THOUGHTS

If I had a few messages to share about my life in my future obituary or memorial book, I'd like them to go something like this:

1 - Pick your spouse and friends based on *kindness*.
You will need that reflective warmth throughout your life.

2 - Try to live without fear. Fear limits joy and blinds us to our options.

3 - Believe in yourself. Even when things aren't quite working—know you have the ability to turn it around.

4 - Learn to listen. There are messages coming your way that can be of help.

5 - Make choices. *If you're not happy,* look around and *choose again*.

PROFESSIONAL PHOTO

And finally, acknowledge the inevitable. None of us are here forever. So, make sure you have at least one professional photograph. Trust me. It'll come in handy someday.

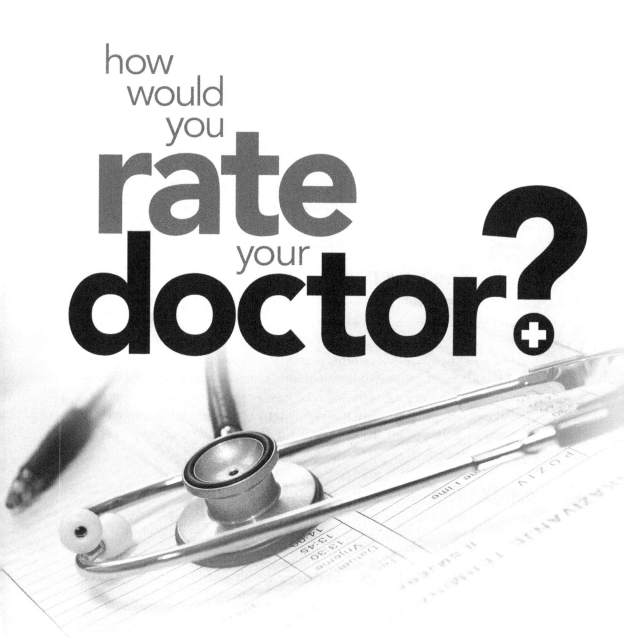

how would you rate your doctor?

THIS WEEK, THE *TOP DOCTORS OF PHOENIX* ARRIVED IN THE MAIL.

Double the thickness of the regular Phoenix Magazine—this sumptuous, four-color special edition is a healthcare bonanza. Every healthcare company in the metropolitan area seems to have paid for advertising space. Insurers, hospitals, private practices, urgent care centers. An impressive compendium of smiling professionals eager to schedule your next appointment.

TOP DOCTORS?

So how do they select the top doctors? The answer: by surveying other doctors. In essence, physicians complete forms indicating whom they believe to be the best physicians. Then, the magazine confirms that each of the recommended physicians is board certified. Finally, names are cross-referenced against the state's records to confirm that there hasn't been any disciplinary action in the last five years.

SURVEYS? BOARD CERTIFIED? DISCIPLINARY ACTION?

During the course of my career, I don't recall many physicians being interested in completing surveys. For one thing, their time is more than absorbed by seeing patients. Physicians' offices are chaotic, busy places. The focus is mostly on the management of the physician's schedule—making sure that patients are being seen in a timely fashion. Board certification? Well, it sounds great—but it's really the standard. Hospitals only affiliate with board-certified doctors or those young physicians on their way to board certification. The same is true for insurance companies. And as for being the subject of disciplinary action, a physician has to do some fairly outrageous stuff before they ever find themselves in that quandary.

SO HOW DO YOU MEASURE QUALITY?

Let's take orthopedic surgery. If you need a knee replacement, you should know how many knees that physician does each year. You should be concerned about the infection rate, readmissions to the hospital, and even the mortality rate. Those statistics offer real insight into a physician's quality of care.

ELECTRONIC MEDICAL RECORDS

In the age of EMRs, that is exactly the kind of data that is sourced. Healthcare and insurance executives have access to it so that they can effectively manage reimbursement from the federal government. But to the consumer, such data remains proprietary. So, until quality data is readily available, instead of looking through a magazine, you're probably better off asking your trusted primary care physician for a referral to a specialist. And as for the magazine? Well, it still looks good on the coffee table.

where?

areallthesedarnpillowscomingfrom

CAN IT BE THAT PILLOWS ARE LIKE RABBITS?

Turn your back for a moment and suddenly two become four? Four become six? Six become eight?

That's how it works in our house. Without trying, we've managed to collect enough pillows to fill a closet. All sorts of pillows. Sofa and decorative bed pillows in every shade and color. Pillows on which to lay your head down at night. Pillows to support your back. King, queen, and regular sizes. All stuffed in one closet. Loaded in so tightly, I can't open the door without pillows tumbling out.

WHY PILLOWS?

We have friends who collect pottery. Others, magnificent glass.
Go to their homes, the pottery and blown glass are on display. Other friends
own wonderful artwork. They have lovely oils and charcoals mounted on the
walls. A few friends are even obsessed with fine china. Sets of dishes to be
used only during the holiday season. Others love Native American artwork.

Okay, I get it. It's wonderful to own beautiful things. Especially if they're family
heirlooms. That all makes sense to me. But pillows?

I BLAME THE MOVING COMPANY

We've moved around a lot in the last few years. Detroit to San Francisco, and
then later on to Phoenix. Each time, we've hired movers to pack us up. At first
it was because we were too busy with our careers to do the packing ourselves.
Then, it was because we were saving our strength for unpacking. Finally, it was
sheer laziness. And somehow, along the way, the pillows began to pile up.
New sofas, new bedding, and inattention to sorting through the excess.

EENIE, MEENIE, MINIE, MO

And so, I've made up my mind. It's time to free up that closet.
Decide what we want to keep and give the rest to charity. We'll face up
to the task. We can use the space. After all, they're just pillows. You can't
make a mistake getting rid of a pillow.

Or can you?

Maybe, on second thought, I should wait. After all, it's the
guest room closet. No one really goes in there. Shut
the door—problem solved. Ah, magical thinking!

lessons
i've
learned
from
my

dog

about
aging

EVERY MORNING AT 6:00 A.M.,

Charlie, our miniature apricot poodle, stands up on the bed and does a brisk shake. It's time to get up and walk the neighborhood. And even though I sometimes want to stay in bed longer, I've come to understand that my dog has a lot to share about growing older. He's already half-way through his fourteenth year, so he knows about aging. I only need to pay a bit of attention to incorporate the lessons.

KEEP MOVING

Charlie walks best in the cool morning hours. And though he might be stiff with the first few steps, he moves amazingly well once he gets going. Walking remains an important part of his day even though he might stumble on an occasional curb. But he doesn't give up.

ADAPT TO YOUR LIMITATIONS

There was a time when Charlie insisted on playing ball every morning. He'd leap and spin, barking and growling enthusiastically. He still plays, but it's limited to one or two tugs on a dog toy. The joy remains, though the activity level is diminished. He indulges in life within the context of his abilities.

IF THIS BUSH DOESN'T WORK OUT—FIND ANOTHER

Charlie seeks out the best information the neighborhood has to offer. He carefully selects where to make his mark and when to leave his scent. Life is all about choices. Charlie knows the excitement of life is often found at the next bush.

NOT EVERY MEAL NEEDS TO BE DEVOURED

There was a time when Charlie ate his meals with gusto. Those days are over. He now eats with a lot of our encouragement. Sitting next to him on the floor has become the routine. Often, we hand feed the first few bites to get him going. Sometimes, we even skip a meal because he's just not interested.

LOVE CAN BE EXPRESSED IN MANY WAYS

Pleasure is all about eye contact. When you're in Charlie's company, he's memorizing every detail of your face. In bed at night, Charlie is a regular hot water bottle. He enjoys looking into our eyes as he gets his nighttime scratch. Then, he plants himself next to you and doesn't move much until the early morning hours.

WHINING IS OKAY

Charlie moans a lot. Getting up, sitting down, or stretching, he seems to always have something to say. We're hoping it's just the normal aches and pains of the aging process. Despite it, he seems none the worse for wear.

COUGHING IS ANOTHER WAY OF SAYING "I'M HERE"

For two years, Charlie has endured congestive heart disease. His heart is so large that it presses on the esophagus, creating a cough. It's purely mechanical, and yet when it first started, we were terrified. But now, it has become his *theme song*. He's adjusted to it and so we have stopped panicking. If he's coughing, he's still around.

NOTHING IS FOREVER

Charlie's time may be limited, but then so is ours. At least for today, we are together and content to enjoy the moment. So, I will get down on the floor and give him another kiss as he studies my face. And isn't that really all any of us have? This one moment? I think so.

if you're a
baby
boomer...

BACK IN THE EARLY 1980S,
I ATTENDED A WORKSHOP AT THE UNIVERSITY OF MICHIGAN.

It was an insightful week. We learned about market research, dived into market analysis, and heard how to create a marketing plan. But the most powerful message wasn't about the tools. It was about Baby Boomers—the people who had the purchasing power. And the message was clear: Young people spend money. Lots of money. Which is why advertisers create messages skewed to a younger audience.

BABY BOOMERS

That once-youthful market of Baby Boomers (26 percent of the United States population) is now well beyond middle age. Each day, 10,000 Boomers turn 65. Imagine, 65! Now, it's true that you can still be a *youthful* 60-something. You can exercise regularly, be sharp-witted, and read voraciously. And you can look fabulous. But there is no way you can really consider yourself *young*. Well, you can, but you might be the only one who does.

SILENCE IS GOLDEN

Now, I like being older. Maybe because when I was younger things didn't always go so well. There were lots of personal challenges to work through. Troubling times that inspired insecurity and doubt. Oh, I still have those moments. I'm sure we all do. But at least now, I understand such feelings are momentary. If age offers wisdom, we learn that not every misstep in life is a calamity. Age helps put that lesson into perspective.

BUT I REALLY WANT TO TELL YOU HOW MUCH I LOVE OLIVE GARDEN

There's a market research firm here in Phoenix that periodically seeks volunteers for research studies. They pay good money for people just like you to share your opinion. Now, when was the last time anyone offered to pay to hear that? To me, that's a dream come true. But lately, I've noticed there are fewer opportunities to participate in the studies. The age category of "60+" is missing. No one seems to be interested in my opinion on colas, laundry detergents, or restaurants. The only surveys that I seem to qualify for: adult diapers, home care services, or Medicare options.

BUT I'M FEELING FINE

Is there a cultural bias that, once you hit a certain age, your opinion is no longer relevant? Or is it merely the expectation that with age, we experience a serious health decline? Where can we find images of vital, vibrant seniors, enjoying the outdoors? Water skiing. Hiking. Running 10Ks. Hurtling through life with effervescence and vitality? Oh, yes. In the AARP magazine. Everyone pictured there is refreshingly perky, smiling, and happy. Gee, I wonder if that magazine sponsors focus group research. Hmm. I'll have to Google that!

why is there so much movie violence

IT'S A PERFECTLY LOVELY SUMMER DAY IN PHOENIX,

and I've just returned from the movies where we go to retreat from the heat once we've dried off from a dip in the pool. But today, I feel rattled, unnerved, unsettled. We've just seen a supposed comedy masquerading as an action film. Don't get me wrong. I'm not a wuss. It's amazing what they can create on film with special effects. The Titanic sinking. New York City flooded. San Francisco imploding.

I GET IT. THEY'RE SPECTACLES, FOR SURE. BUT WHAT IS IT WITH ALL THE VIOLENCE?

Human beings being mowed down in a bloody shooting spree. Body parts chopped off, flying through the air. The continuous violence goes on and on. And that's just in the previews.

THE THREE STOOGES

When I was growing up, violence was limited to *The Three Stooges.* Three knuckleheads who couldn't stop hitting each other. Yes, we laughed. Pies in the face, okay. But punches to the gut, pokes to the eye, followed by a hammer to the head? Looking back, I wonder why more kids didn't accidentally kill their siblings imitating a *Three Stooges* episode. I can just hear the excuses: "But Moe whacked Curley in the face with an iron skillet!" Or "Larry never cried when his hair was ripped out of his head!" Or, God forbid, "Shemp fell out a window and he seemed fine."

I KNOW THE VIOLENCE ISN'T REAL

Back then, it all seemed innocent. It was done for comic relief. But today, the violence feels intensely real. There's nothing comedic about it. Your body tenses up as you watch it. It's like being on a thrill ride, except it goes on and on. Lately, I've worried that this is a minority opinion. Surely Hollywood isn't in the business of making movies no one wants to see. They're merely feeding the box office. Or are they leading it?

IS OUR SOCIETY OUT OF CONTROL?

Anyone who wants to get all revved up can just turn to the news or social media to quicken their heartbeat. When I go to the movies, I'd prefer to escape. A love story would be nice. A rom-com to make me laugh and remember how wonderful falling in love can be. Maybe even a movie that sparks the intellect. How about a thoughtful biography? Or a tale of friendship?

Honestly, I'm exhausted by the political rancor that is our daily diet in America. I'd like to give my flight-or-fight response a rest. Wouldn't you? Wouldn't most Americans?

why
can't
we
bequeth
our
friends
when
we

die?

RIP

MY DEAR FRIEND HAROLD RECENTLY PASSED AWAY.

He was a lovely guy whose friends rallied to his side in his time of need.
Harold was in the hospital for weeks and he was never alone. Friends circled
like *Care Bears*. And as I watched the love, I came to realize the importance of
setting down long-term roots in a community. Friendships that span decades
with people who truly love you. You see, Harold was born and raised in
Detroit, and unlike the generations that followed, many of his core friends
had remained anchored to that city. Their children had grown up there with
Uncle Harold.

BLOOD IS THICKER THAN WATER

Not always. And in Harold's case, I'd say the opposite was true. Yes, he had a family who loved him, but they had long ago moved away. His real family had morphed from the offspring of these long-term friendships. Young people in whom Harold had invested time and attention. The infants that he'd once held in his arms came to sit by his Detroit bedside to hold his hand. The commitments were real. The connections were unbroken by time or distance.

STANDING STILL

There's a lot to be said for staying in one place. It certainly provides a greater stability to cement relationships. And as I watched all these Detroit friends, I wondered how they'd managed to remain Detroiters. I'd long ago succumbed to the siren call of San Francisco and then on to Phoenix. Years spent pursuing other friends, other dreams, while many of my Detroit friends had also left to settle in Southern California. I'd come to believe that *you have friends for a season and friends for a reason* and that there was always an opportunity to make new friends. I hadn't thought about life's emergencies. The events that knock us to our knees. The times when we really need those special connections.

THE INTERSECT

In my debut novel, *The Intersect,* I wrote about Daisy, a septuagenarian, who suddenly finds herself alone during a healthcare crisis. As I stood in Harold's hospital room in Detroit, I wondered if my character Daisy was motivated more about my own fear than I had dared to admit to myself. Was I afraid that one day I might be at the mercy of strangers, no family and friends to support me? In the novel, Daisy gets lucky. Caring and wonderful people step up to rescue her. Perhaps that's my truest wish—a wish Harold never had to consider because he'd already done the hard work to ensure that he'd not be alone. He'd loved his friends unconditionally. His friends *had become his family.*

WE ALL HAVE FRIENDS

It's just too bad that, along with money and worldly possessions, we can't bequeath the amazing people in our lives to someone else whom we love. I'd have considered myself immensely lucky to have inherited as a friend any of the fine people who surrounded Harold in his last few weeks. He was blessed and I will dearly miss him, but until the end of my days, I will remember the crowd that gathered in his hospital room. For a brief moment, I was part of something amazing. Something rare and special. Adults gathered at the bedside of a dear friend as if he were part of their immediate family. For, you see, he was the *chosen family member.*

here a

psychic,

there a

psychic,

everywhere a

psychic,

psychic!

PHOENIX HAS BEEN OVERRUN.

And I'm not referring to ants. Though, if you leave food on your counters, ants will surely show up. I'm referring to psychics. In Phoenix, there seems to be one on every corner. Find a Starbucks—find a psychic. Tarot cards, horoscopes, palm and aura readings. The spiritually gifted must love the warm weather.

CALLING THE DEAD. CALLING THE DEAD. COME IN, THE DEAD.

On television, there's been an explosion of psychic talent, too. Theresa Caputo from Long Island says she can connect to the other side. Heck, I grew up in Queens, which is technically on Long Island. No one seemed psychic back then. Crazy, yes. But psychic? No.

And then there's baby-faced Tyler Henry. He provides readings to television's reality stars. He swears that he has no idea who these Hollywood celebrities are. Frankly, neither do I. Perhaps I should buy a copy of *People* magazine every now and then.

Then there is a *Psychic Taxi*. This show makes sense to me. I like the idea of connecting to the other side while stuck in traffic. Why not? I've got time to kill.

A TRUE BELIEVER WRAPPED IN A CYNIC'S SOUL

Now don't be fooled. I may seem a cynic. But I'm a cynic hoping someday to be convinced. It would be great to know that my loved ones are looking out for me. That somehow, through the process of crossing-over, they've become more loving, enlightened, and accepting people. Gosh. That would be a dream come true.

AND NOW FOR THE SKEPTIC...

So, why would I need a third party to contact my dearly departed? God knows they were never shy when they were alive. I'm sure if I just stopped and listened, I could hear their voices in my head. My mother would say she loves me and is proud of the man I've become. My father would apologize for behaving like such an ass when he married that wealthy widow after my mother died. I can hear them both now. Now, when their words would have no impact on my life. Or would they? Hmm. Does anyone know a good psychic?

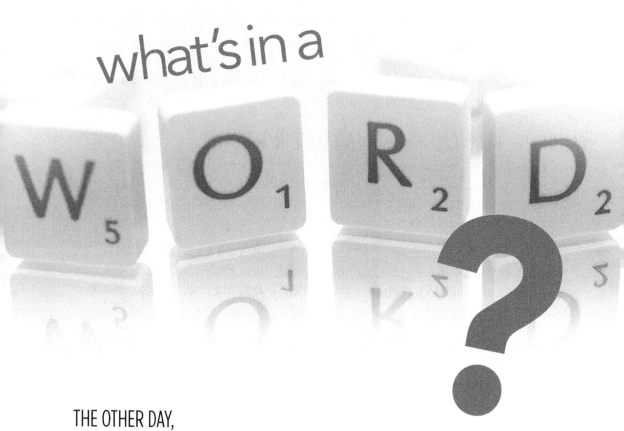

what's in a WORD?

THE OTHER DAY,

I was watching an old movie and it occurred to me that a lot of words are no longer in vogue. For instance, "pocketbook." No one uses that word anymore. My grandmother did, but then she's been gone since 1972.

OR "VALISE."

When was the last time anyone packed a valise? Valises are now the exclusive property of Goodwill and certain resale shops. Some have even been refurbished and used as stylized decor in high-end retail settings such as Manhattan's ABC Home Furnishings at 881 Broadway. If you haven't been there, it's worth the trip. It's like stepping back in time. Everything old is new again! Especially the way the merchandise is displayed. During my last visit a few years back, they had rows of restored school lockers. Nostalgia alone tempted me to nearly make a purchase.

DARLING, HOLD ME CLOSE!

And when was the last time someone uttered those words? Greta Garbo, Joan Crawford, Bette Davis? It sure isn't happening in my house. Darling seems to have gone the way of Post Toasties, *Dark Victory,* and Tallulah Bankhead. We've become a society of "babe," "sweetie," and "dear." Now, I admit, I like the sound of darling. It's romantic. And there is nothing wrong with romance. Come to think of it, I'd prefer my darlings to be whispered in the dark and behind closed doors. I know. That's highly unlikely. So, in the interim, *honey* will just have to do.

THE CHIROPODIST HAS A MISTRESS?

A chiropodist was once the professional name for a podiatrist. Today, you won't find a shingle boasting the services of a chiropodist. Too bad. Chiropodist is such an interesting word. It has a musical quality. Chiropodist! I imagine happy toes wiggling with excitement. And, talking about excitement, does a rich married guy still have a mistress? I think the sexual revolution and the women's movement have done away with that classification. And to be fair, when was the last time anyone was called a gigolo? I'm drawing a blank.

PARTNER?

Which brings me to the term partner. In my novel *After the Fall,* a misunderstanding arises between Harry, a guy in his mid-50s, and Barney, a teenager, when the word partner is invoked. For the older character, the term "partner" is a substitute for a "gay spouse." For the teenager, though, it sounds like two fellows in business together. I have to admit, even as a married man, I sometimes default to the word partner. Old habits die hard, while new words require practice. I guess it really is all about being comfortable with change. Harry and I seem to share that struggle. But I'm working on it. And I guess that's really all we can ask of ourselves.

By the way, if you haven't met my husband, Jeff, he's one hell of a guy!

trauma
and
humor

IF YOU FOLLOW ME ON FACEBOOK,

then you might have guessed there would be an upcoming blog about the passing of our sweet poodle, Charlie. He would have been fifteen years old in December, which is a good run for any dog. He'd been sick for the last two and a half years with congestive heart disease, and though Jeff and I were aware that time was running out, the shock of his passing was still overwhelming.

OH, NO. YOU'RE NOT GOING TO TALK ABOUT IT?

Yes. Just a bit. Bear with me.

OUR FIRST DOG

In 2002, I was out of town on business when Jeff put Woody, our wirehaired fox terrier, to sleep. And even though it was many years ago, I remember being relieved that I didn't have to make the decision. Poor Jeff had to do it alone. And, to be honest, I didn't understand the pain of the experience. I wasn't in the room that day. I didn't hold Woody as he took his last breath. It was easy to separate from the experience. Easy for me to make ridiculous jokes in a pathetic attempt to lighten the mood. After all, that's what I do. When things get uncomfortable, I joke. It's my coping strategy.

AND NOW THIS WEEK

We opted for in-home euthanasia after the vet told us that Charlie needed daily doses of fluids under the skin. We were familiar with the procedure. We'd given fluids to our first dog for over six months. Woody never seemed to mind. He always sat calmly through it and then immediately perked up. But Charlie was not about to do the same. He'd had enough. I could see it in his eyes. We were scaring him, and he was tired. Too many pills and too much poking.

IT WAS TIME

And so, Jeff and I decided together, and our vet agreed. We opted for an in-home visit, thinking it would be easier for Charlie. But there is no such thing as "easier" when it comes to euthanasia. I'm still haunted by the surprised look in Charlie's eyes when he was poked in the rear by the first needle, the drug that provided the calming euphoria. And then his look when he received the last shot. And those final breaths.

APOLOGIES ARE DUE

At times in our lives we seem to create discord in our relationships without really understanding how. I did that by not appreciating the extent of the trauma Jeff suffered when he put Woody to sleep, while I was away. I under-stand that pain now. Sometimes, we need to go through an experience to grasp the enormity of its impact. I wish that weren't true. And for that, I am sorry. Jeff deserved better.

trick
or treat

STEP AWAY FROM THE CANDY BOWL!

WITH HALLOWEEN JUST AROUND THE CORNER,

this is the time of year when we make that dreaded purchase: candy. Lots of candy. It's on special everywhere. Bags and bags. Gooey, chewy, crunchy, stick-to-your-dental-work stuff. And each year, we try to pick candy that we don't like. This is hard to do! For, each year, we're reminded that there isn't much that we actually dislike.

CHOCOLATE VS. MARSHMELLOW

In our house, there are two teams: Chocolate Lovers (me) and Marshmallow Mavens (Jeff). This, of course, means that any candy including either ingredient is out of the running for Halloween. Our philosophy: Don't bring into the house *anything* that either of us might like to snack on. Standing in front of the candy aisle at the supermarket, we can be overheard having that exact discussion. Small children have been known to shun us.

BUT CANDY IS EVERYWHERE

When I go to the bank (notice—I didn't say "the ATM"), there is usually a big stash of candy to pick through as you wait in line. I think this significantly improves customer service. Especially when I see Reese's Peanut Butter Cups. God outdid himself the day he prompted H. B. Reese to resign from Hershey and create a new candy company. Combining chocolate and peanut butter was pure genius!

BACK TO THE SUPERMARKET

And so, the challenge is once again before us. What should we buy that we both won't eat? In the past, we've opted for Butterfingers. Nestle describes the candy as a crunchy peanut butter core covered in chocolate. Sounds delicious. But there is something about the dry texture that bothers me. Plus, it gets caught up in your teeth like toffee or taffy. Dentists must love it.

BUT ARE WE REALLY BEING FAIR TO THE LITTLE CHILDREN?

After all, Halloween is about the kids. Shouldn't we be giving out candy that we think the little tykes will love? Candy that is truly delicious? M&M's, Plain and Peanut. Milky Ways. Snickers. What can be the harm in buying those wonderful treats?

WE ALL DESERVE A LITTLE HALLOWEEN FUN

So, this year, things will be different. Instead of buying the candy we like the least, we're going to purchase the candy we love the best. And then, *we'll try to remember to turn on the outside porch lights on October 31st.* And no matter how loud the television is blasting, *we'll listen for the doorbell.* Heck, we might even stay in that night instead of going to a movie. Who knows? Trick or treat—and the best of the evening to you and yours—and to all the little children.

the traveling
big head
show

COMING TO A THEATER NEAR YOU

IT HAPPENED AGAIN:

We have tickets to a show. We're comfortably seated with a great view of the stage. And then, just before the lights dim, the giant head arrives. We're not disappointed. We know the giant head. It follows us from theater to theater, forever blocking our view.

TALL MEN

When God made tall men, he should have made adjustable seats.
Especially if the big galoot hasn't learned to slouch. Personally, I try to
sit on my lower back, thrusting my shoulders forward and down. It takes
inches off. It's awkward but courteous. And my chiropractor says it has done
wonders for his bank account.

THE BOOK OF MORMON

I've *not seen* this show on Broadway. Oh, yes. I was in the theater for the
performance. Sitting behind a stocky gentleman. Let's call him Moose. Moose
once played college football. His neck—the size of a tree trunk. His ears stuck
out. I should have saved my money and bought the cast album because that's
how I experienced the show: a concert in a darkened room.

KINKY BOOTS

Girl, she's got some wild boots! At least that's what I heard. This time, we
were in London sitting in the "stalls." That's England's answer to ground level
seating. I shifted back and forth in rhythm to the guy in front of me, who kept
leaning this way and that. The show should have been called *Kinky Boat.* At
the end, I felt seasick.

WHAT'S A FELLA TO DO?

Yes, I know. There are worse things in life. But when you pay good money
for theater tickets, you hope to actually see the show. Come to think of it—
who designed those itty-bitty seats? Does anyone's tush really fit in them?
The velvet almost makes it impossible to shift about. And what are you supposed to do with your knees? All good thoughts to occupy your mind the next
time the big-headed galoot shows up. And he will. He hasn't missed
a performance yet!

thanks
giving
turkey or not

IT'S TURKEY TIME AGAIN,

and so the hoopla begins about how to defrost the darn bird without poisoning your family. Throughout the year, Americans might eat turkey, but mostly in a different form: ground turkey, cutlets, breasts, or luncheon meat. Preparing the whole bird is strictly a Thanksgiving Day endeavor.

And so, on this one day of the year, the threat looms: defrost that bird correctly, or suffer the consequences. And I don't mean your Aunt Martha's disapproval.

WHAT? NO TURKEY?

Years ago, I found myself at a restaurant for a family Thanksgiving celebration. My in-laws had decided to have Thanksgiving at a rib joint. Now, I love ribs, but really? Thanksgiving is for turkey. Preferably a big buffet loaded with every possible carb that your cardiologist has warned against. That's my idea of a celebration. And I'm sure most Americans would agree. How did I resolve the dilemma? The following week, we prepared a traditional meal at home. And so, with just the two of us, turkey became our main staple. Lots of turkey. Just enough for us to get good and sick of the whole thing. And that must be the reason why Thanksgiving comes only once every 365 days. Who can tolerate the leftovers?

SIDE DISHES

Let's face it. The sides make the meal. Sweet potatoes, green bean casserole, stuffing. But then comes the traditional pumpkin pie. I don't like pumpkin. Whoever came up with that idea must have been asleep at the stove. I say, keep the pumpkin for the jack-o'-lantern and make another dessert. I'd welcome a nice cheesecake, fruit pie, or brownie. And I find that ice cream can really help one's digestion. A big scoop always does the trick.

HAVE A GREAT CELEBRATION

So, from our family to yours, here's wishing you a terrific Thanksgiving. Enjoy the meal and your family and friends. And remember. It's not "all about the food." By the way, would you pass the gravy? What do you mean there's no gravy?

whatever happened to customer service ?

CUSTOMER SERVICE IS DISAPPEARING.

Now, I'm not talking about the salesperson who waits on you at the store. That person has been missing in action for years. No. I'm talking about the ability to pick up a phone and solve a problem directly. For some reason, it's becoming increasingly impossible to find an actual telephone number to call. In many cases, that kind of customer service no longer exists.

TWILIGHT ZONE

I get that we live in the digital age and "technology is our friend." On so many levels, I agree. Who doesn't like to order online? Or Skype? Or read my blog? Okay—maybe that's pushing it. But technology is now part of how we live. Release the resistance! Let's all take a breath.

But there's a downside, too.

Life has become 24/7. We're always on. There's no escaping the iPhone. Texts arrive. Emails must be answered. The work week has stretched beyond office hours. And I guess that's okay, because we now have Netflix and YouTube and Twitter and Facebook. The world is at our fingertips. Goodie.

BUT WHERE'S THE CUSTOMER SERVICE NUMBER?

So why can't I get hold of anyone in customer service?

The technology companies were the first to do away with "live" customer service. Have a problem with your computer? There's a chat box to start a dialogue. Problems with your website host? There are online "help" videos to scour through. Okay—I get it. I don't like it, but I get it. It's like the healthcare companies of the 1980s that insisted that you not smoke on their premises. It has to start somewhere.

But recently I noticed that even my cell phone provider has done away with the customer service number. Checking through the newly formatted bill, the number is gone. I guess everyone in America is satisfied with their service.

HOW IRONIC

When I complain—and, despite the rumors, it's not very often—I want to talk with a living, breathing human being. I want some high-touch with my high-tech. I don't think that's a lot to ask. And I don't want to have to search high and low for the customer service number. Or click through a complicated series of links. Customer service should always be readily available from any company in the "business of business." And I'd share that opinion directly … if only I could find a place to post comments on the business's homepage. Yeesh!

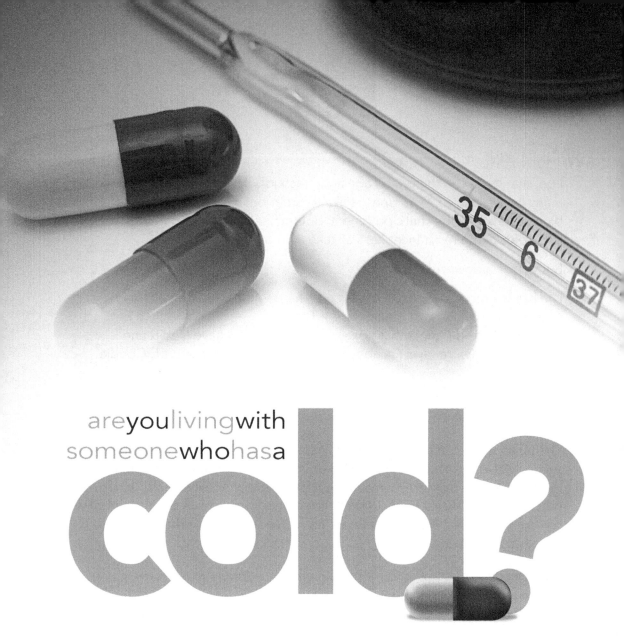

areyoulivingwith
someonewhohasa

cold?

IT'S THAT TIME OF YEAR.

The cold and flu season. And even though I've had my flu shot, the greatest risk of getting sick isn't from exposure to the general public. No, the greatest risk is the big lunk lying next to me in bed, sharing my living quarters, and coughing. I won't name names, but you all know to whom I'm referring. And yes, he's sick this week.

EVER SINCE *CAPTAIN KANGAROO*

As a kid, I was sick a lot. And *Mrs. Doctor Know-It-All Mommy* was the queen of over-the-counter medications. Robitussin for coughs. Vicks VapoRub for the chest. Afrin for the sinuses. For dinner, she prepared a meal packed with iron. Have you guessed it yet? That's right. A disgusting slab of rubbery, stringy, hold-your-nose calf's liver. *Mrs. Doctor Know-It-All Mommy* was no gourmet chef when it came to preparing liver. And if you're thinking of sharing a terrific recipe with me, please don't. I say, let the calf have its liver. I'll stick with the chicken's soup.

WHY AM I DIZZY?

So now, I have an aversion to medication. Too often, the stuff makes me dizzy. And I've read that a frequent cause of death in adults (okay—it might really be seniors) is a sudden fall that results in a head injury. As for the liver, well, things have slightly changed. I like rumaki, paté, and chopped liver, but I still think plain liver is gross. Now everyone knows what not to serve if I ever come over for dinner.

FEED A COLD, STARVE A FEVER

Excellent advice. I'm so enthusiastic about it that I enjoy regularly practicing the *feeding* part. You can never be too prepared. But seriously, to ward off being sick, experts recommend that you wash your hands frequently with hot water. I'm not happy till my hands are raw. And you must avoid touching your eyes, nose, and mouth. Which of course leaves your fingers with actually very little to do. But, most importantly, isolate your beloved to another room. Or wear one of those face masks seen at airports. Better yet, make your spouse wear the mask.

USE YOUR SMART PHONE

Limit all communication with your spouse to texting to him or her in the next room. It cuts down on the germ exposure. And there are lots of great emojis and GIFs to use. My bottom-line advice: Tap into your creative side, and stay healthy!

COMPLAINING IS AN AWFUL BEHAVIOR.

Especially when it's done without consideration for the poor person who has to listen to you. Complaining to someone who is financially strapped about the problems you're having scheduling that European trip is rude, at best.

Crabbing about the service at a restaurant when the waiter is rushing about like a madman—I consider that also to be insensitive. Grousing about Washington, D.C.—well, that's just the norm. But complaining for the sake of hearing your own voice—now, that's a problem.

NOT YOU AGAIN?

No one wants to listen to a lot of whining about nothing. Certainly not in my house. Or so I've been told on more than one occasion. Okay, maybe over one hundred times. After that, I stopped counting. And that was back in 1991.

My *updates*—as I like to call them—tend to focus on how I'm feeling. I'm acutely aware of every little ache or pain. Not that they're major. They're not. But I like to keep Jeff *updated*. I'm being considerate. Just in case something does happen—he should have the necessary information for the EMTs.

FAMILY, HOLD BACK

I've learned through the years to shield my friends from these *updates*. Right now, some are rolling their eyes and laughing—but don't you believe them. The real *updating* has been heaped squarely on Jeff's shoulders. Mostly in the morning. Usually when he's checking his iPhone. Or does he start checking his phone when I start *updating*? Hmm. It's kind of hard to know.

THE BOTTOM LINE

If you want to have friends, don't be a downer. Take a page from my book. Limit your *updates* to the morning—preferably on your way to the bathroom. And as you wobble along, wondering why your balance is off and your feet hurt, hold this thought: It isn't what you say that's important, it's the fact that you've said it. You've put it out to the universe. You're alive for another day. And that is the most important *update* of all.

a new year:

HOORAY OR OY VEY?

IT'S ANOTHER NEW YEAR AND THAT MEANS A FRESH START.

All things are possible as we look ahead. But, to be honest, that just isn't my nature. I tend to be the guy looking over his shoulder, wondering what could have been. All right. I know, that's a bit of a downer. But we can't all be running around happily celebrating. I'd call that chaos. So instead of spreading New Year's cheer, I'm going to share my private thoughts about the New Year. Just consider it another perspective.

GUY LOMBARDO VS. RYAN SEACREST

Ryan Seacrest is a personable guy. And Anderson Cooper and Andy Cohen can also be fun to watch. But really, I miss Guy Lombardo and the live telecast from the Waldorf Astoria. I know: Corny, perhaps. But there was something special about watching New York's high society celebrating in the Grand Ballroom. It was like sitting on the stairs in your pajamas looking in on the adults partying in the living room below. Everything seemed so elegant. And we just don't do elegant anymore.

IT'S A WONDERFUL LIFE

And what happened to all those terrific holiday films? Yes, *The Wizard of Oz* had a telecast. Thank goodness. But nowhere else on TV could you find *The Miracle on 34th Street*, or *It's a Wonderful Life*, or *Holiday Inn*. I checked Turner Movie Classics on Christmas Day. These beloved films have been replaced by modern fare. Okay, I get it. Time marches on. Maybe so. But I haven't.

JANUARY BIRTHDAY

It might be easier if I weren't a Capricorn. Being a "Cappy" means I must come to grips with both the New Year and my growing a year older, all within days of each other.

My cake now holds only one candle. No sense in setting off the smoke alarm. I can make a wish and easily blow it out with one breath. I'm surrounded by birthday cards with jokes about indigestion, arthritis, and flatulence. The cards make me laugh even though they portend a scary future. One that we all seem to fear.

ONE STEP FORWARD, TWO STEPS BACK

So, for me, New Year's is less about *Auld Lang Syne* and more about the *Hokey Pokey*. It will take months before I'm comfortable with the New Year. Some of us are just slow adapters. Nonetheless, I still want to wish everyone a happy and healthy New Year. Just don't make me say the exact year.

ten More tips
for a happy life

A FEW MONTHS BACK,
I WROTE A BLOG ABOUT BEING HAPPY.

Now, for those of you who know me, that might come as a surprise. I don't seem to put out that kind of energy. I'm not known as a happy-go-lucky type of guy. I'm more of a worrier. Like Dave in my debut novel, *The Intersect,* I tend to live in the land of regret. Always looking backward and wondering if I've made the right choices.

GLASS HALF-FULL?

Now, don't get me wrong. It's not that I've never experienced happiness. I have. But I think the problem may be my expectation of what happiness feels like. For instance, on a good day, when everything is clicking, I feel calm and relaxed. No—I'm not smiling from ear to ear, or running around giving hugs, or laughing wildly. Instead, I feel a sense that I'm on the right path. I tend to experience happiness as inner satisfaction. Nothing to fret about today? Ah. "Good day. Me happy!"

So today, I thought I'd share my coping strategies when faced with life's little bugaboos. The things that drive me crazy and the solutions that I've devised to let go of the negative energy. I'll just cover a few for your consideration. They're simple and don't require much explanation. If they make you smile... then I've done my job.

SO HOW DO I KEEP MY SPIRITS UP?

1 THERE'S HUMOR TO BE HAD IN EVERYTHING WE DO.

Look for the funny side. And if something strikes your funny bone, share it. Laughter is contagious. It attracts people to you. Just like a good antiperspirant.

2 DON'T BE AFRAID TO SHOW EMOTION.

People feel closer to you when they experience you as real. And yes, crying is necessary. Tears are healing. But be judicious. The cashier on the "10 items or less" line at the supermarket has only so much time to listen to your woes. Trust me. I know from personal experience.

3 BE MORE LIKE FRED ASTAIRE.

Dance when you're alone! It lifts your spirits. Even if you're as clumsy as an ox, dancing is a great way to cheer yourself up…as well as entertain the dog.

4 MIRRORS ARE BEST ENJOYED WHEN YOU MAKE SILLY FACES.

So, go ahead and make a face. Then think about which member of your family you look like. I can make the same faces as my late grandfather. It's always nice to see him staring back at me.

5 LAUGH LINES ENHANCE YOUR NATURAL GOOD LOOKS.

At the very least, they add character. So, let them be.

6 EXERCISE IS INVIGORATING. *(UNTIL IT ISN'T.)*

Allow your body time to heal before you blow out your knee—hip—elbow—lower back—Achilles tendon.

7 IF YOU DON'T LIKE THE WAY YOU LOOK, STOP LOOKING AT YOURSELF.

Turn your gaze to someone you love, and enjoy the view.

8 WRITING A LETTER CAN BE THERAPEUTIC.

Seeing a trained therapist is far more effective. What we pay for tends to hold greater value.

9 LOVING YOURSELF MAY BE THE MOST IMPORTANT LESSON OF ALL.

But acting like the center of the universe? Well, no one likes that.

AND NOW… *HERE'S SOMETHING FOR THE SOUL. TIP #10.*

10 YOU BECOME WHAT YOU FOCUS ON.

Years ago, I decided to become a writer, and I kept that dream firmly in mind, and then worked on it steadily. You, too, can be and do anything you want. It's all within your reach. Well, not immediately—but with persistence. So, if you don't like what's going on in your life, choose again. Anything is possible.

in
conclusion

DID YOU ENJOY READING
*WHAT'S THAT GROWING
IN MY SOUR CREAM*

?

if so, then **please:**

1 Rate the book on *AMAZON.COM* and *GOODREADS.COM*

2 Join brad Graber's email list at *www.bradgraber.com* and receive his blog: *There, I Said It!*

3 Consider giving this book as a gift to family and friends

4 Recommend the book to your local book club

5 Mention you loved the book on your social media platform, using the hashtag *#SourCream*

6 Write a review on your blog

7 Follow Brad Graber on social media: *Twitter @Jefbra1* and *Like* Brad Graber's author page on *Facebook*

8 And, more importantly, check out Brad's two books of award-winning contemporary fiction: *The Intersect* and *After the Fall*

THE INTERSECT

When life veers off course, strangers find comfort and lasting connection

A NOVEL

BRAD GRABER

IF A STRANGER KNOCKED ON YOUR DOOR WOULD YOU WELCOME THEM IN?

**TALES OF THE CITY MEETS AS GOOD AS IT GETS
IN THIS HEARTWARMING NOVEL ABOUT LOVE AND
FRIENDSHIP AMONG STRANGERS WHO SHOW
UP IN EACH OTHER'S LIVES AT JUST
THE RIGHT MOMENT.**

*"Romance, human connection, the link between the living and the dead ...
punctuated by humorous episodes that will keep the reader
entertained. This is a story that rings with originality; it is
well-crafted and exhilarating."* —**Readers' Favorite**

*"Beautifully told by Brad Graber ... it was only when I closed the book that I
realized I had only been reading."* —**Reviews by Amos Lassen**

Winner of a **National Indie Excellence Award, Readers Favorite Award,**
and **Arizona Authors Association Award.**

 FOR THE FIRST 2 CHAPTERS OF

1

....

US Airways Flight #610 took a sharp bounce, jostling Dave Greenway in his seat. It was the 6:00 a.m. flight out of San Francisco to Phoenix. The scent of freshly brewed coffee wafted through the first-class cabin as he planted his size tens firmly on the floor beneath him, hoping against hope, to stabilize the Airbus 320.

It didn't work.

The plane took another nasty hop.

As Dave struggled to hold his cup steady, coffee splashed everywhere. "Dammit, I knew that was going to happen," he muttered, his hand soaked as he downed the last of the liquid.

Again, the plane bucked hard.

A woman nearby let out a muffled cry. Everyone else fell dead silent. An elderly gentleman emerged from the first-class restroom, zipper down, a surprised look on his face, the front of his khakis wet. As he stumbled to his seat, the unlatched door swung freely. A stewardess jumped up to secure it, balancing herself precariously with one hand on the cockpit door.

Perfect, Dave thought, turning a ghostly white. He pulled his seat belt tighter. *We leave earthquake country and die in a plane crash.*

Seated beside him, his partner Charlie nudged him with an elbow. "It's just a little turbulence," he said confidently. "There's nothing to worry about. Hey, check this out." He held up an old issue of *People* that he'd lifted from the airplane magazine rack. Ryan Reynolds offered a seductive stare.

"Very nice," Dave said dryly, still unnerved by the plane's erratic motion. He searched Charlie's angular face for any sign of tension. "How can you be so calm?"

"Thermal inversion," Charlie said, as he returned to perusing the magazine. "It happens over the desert. If you're scared, just look down at your sweater."

For the big travel day, Dave had worn his favorite black pullover, purchased on a whim at a Greg Norman sale. It contrasted nicely with the silver coursing through his mostly dark hair which he wore conservatively parted on the side. The cotton/poly blend with a zippered collar at the neck, sported the signature shark logo encircled by Norman's motto— *Attack Life*—an attitude Dave admired. Dave loved the primary colors of the shark logo and wondered if it was the designer's nod to the rainbow flag.

The plane jumped side-to-side. Dave gripped the armrests.

"There's no point freaking out," Charlie said, still reading, oblivious to the motion, the dark-grey wispy curls atop his head indifferent to Dave's need for order. "Think of it like riding a roller-coaster. Go with the flow. Tensing up only creates sore muscles."

Dave tried to relax. If Charlie was so blasé, there couldn't be any real danger. After all, Charlie had logged hundreds of thousands of air miles. "I take paradise and put up a parking lot," he'd told Dave when they'd met some twenty years earlier at a Human Rights Campaign Fund Dinner. Dave had returned a blank stare as Charlie, tall, tanned, and dapper in a black tux, explained that he worked with developers on site locations for new stores. Since then, Dave had watched Charlie ricochet around the country, providing market research to support trade area development for retailers, investment banks, and anyone who needed predictive sales modeling.

Charlie closed the *People* magazine. He looked over at Dave. "March is really a great time to move to Phoenix. The weather's ideal. And I can finally say goodbye to all those flight delays at SFO. *No more morning fog.*" He practically sang the last few words.

The motion of the plane calmed as Dave assumed Charlie's joyous mood. "No more jumbo mortgage on that tiny Mill Valley house we once called home."

Charlie's hazel green eyes lit up. "Good riddance to those break-the-bank California taxes."

"Adieu to the rain that arrives in November and stays until April. And a fond farewell to those outrageous gasoline prices."

Charlie smiled. "We're going to save a shitload of money."

"We will," Dave agreed as the plane unexpectedly lost altitude. Dave's gut pressed hard against the seat belt. A second later, his bottom reunited with the cushion, and the mood turned serious. "Beware the Ides of March," he mumbled.

"What the hell does that mean?" Charlie asked, perplexed by the ominous reference.

Dave had no trouble explaining. He'd already given it considerable thought. "Gay people flock to San Francisco. Everyone wants to live in the Bay Area. And here we're leaving. And tomorrow, March 15th of all days, I start my new job."

Charlie sought a positive spin. "With scientists predicting *the next big one*, we'd have been crazy to stay. If our home had been destroyed in an earthquake, we'd have still been on the hook to pay off that huge mortgage."

"True," Dave said, impressed by Charlie's ability to turn the argument. "An earthquake is a terrific strategy to minimize overcrowding in the Bay Area," Dave laughed. "But moving to Arizona . . . *a red state?*"

"How do you think red states turn blue?" Charlie's eyes twinkled. "Pioneers like us. One day we'll look back and say, remember when Arizona was red?"

Dave relented. "I guess that's one way to look at it."

"Sure. And there's a large gay community in Phoenix." Charlie reached down and retrieved his black leather briefcase. Unzipping the front pocket, he pulled out a full-color *Phoenix Homes* magazine. "You have to check out these properties," he said thumbing through the pages. "I've already hooked up with a realtor to show us around."

"Show *you* around," Dave corrected. "I'll be in the office tomorrow. Physician practices need to be managed. From now on, my life will be one long operations meeting, physicians in the morning, physicians at night."

"Well, you took the lead in getting us settled in the Bay Area when we left Michigan. Now it's my turn. God knows I'll have plenty of time. With credit frozen, consumer spending down . . . retail's in such a deep slump. Last Christmas was a real bust. I don't think 2010 will be much better. I should have plenty of time to get us set up. There's not much business on my plate at the moment."

Dave felt bad for Charlie. He'd worked so hard to build a successful business. "Well, Obama really pulled us back from the brink," Dave said, still uncertain that the worst of it was over.

"With so many Americans out of work, it's more like a depression than a recession," Charlie observed glumly. "But we should look on the bright side. With such high employment . . . you have a new job. That's freaking amazing."

"It feels really out of step," Dave agreed, still ambivalent about his good fortune. "Kind of unsettling."

"You're nuts. You should be ecstatic."

"I'm too on edge. I have all these crazy thoughts running through my head," Dave admitted, a nervous tingling shooting through his body.

Charlie gave Dave his full attention. "Tell me. I want to hear."

"It's ridiculous," Dave admitted, blushing. "It's too silly."

"Tell me," Charlie insisted. "I want to know."

Dave relented. He hoped Charlie would be understanding. "Okay. Take my car. It's black with a black interior."

"And?" Charlie asked, stifling a laugh.

Dave continued. "It gets brutally hot in Phoenix during the summer. Black retains the heat."

Charlie offered a huge smile. "You're kidding, right? You know you can't get incinerated driving to work." His voice dripped with sarcasm. "There's such a thing as air conditioning. And if it's a real problem, you'll trade that car in for a white one. Problem solved. What else?"

Dave hesitated.

"What else, what else?" Charlie probed, eager to hear the next concern.

Dave took a deep breath. "You know I'm susceptible to nosebleeds. It's dry in Arizona. I read on the Internet that it's the nosebleed capital of the world."

Charlie gave Dave a sidelong glance. "Now you're making that one up."

"I read it," Dave insisted.

"Your body will adjust," Charlie promised. "You'll be fine. So that's what's worrying you? Here I thought you had concerns about the job."

"I should have kept it to myself. Real men never share," Dave sharply remarked.

Charlie placed a hand on Dave's thigh and gave it a gentle squeeze. "Real men who love each other do. Why not look on the bright side? We'll have domestic partner benefits. For the first time, I can get health insurance through you. No more HMO. Hello, Blue Cross Blue Shield."

"Yeah, that is pretty progressive," Dave agreed, "And of all places . . . Arizona."

"That's what happens when you stop working for Catholic organizations."

"True."

"And the roof won't leak. It barely ever rains in Phoenix. And . . . get ready . . . here it comes . . . we can buy a *new house*. We could never afford that in the Bay Area."

Dave perked up. Images of Sub-Zeros, marble countertops, pebbletech pools, and flagstone patios danced in his head. "A new house . . . wouldn't that be something?"

"We can do whatever we want," Charlie answered, once again opening the *People* magazine and flipping through the pages.

Dave looked over Charlie's shoulder. "My God," he said, pointing at a photo of Gilles Marini. "He looks a bit like you when you were young. You had the same five o'clock shadow and all that jet-black hair."

"I was hot," Charlie agreed. "But if I worked out like you," Charlie rubbed his tummy, "I'd probably drop these last ten pounds."

"Hey, I'm at the gym to manage stress," Dave emphasized, explaining his obsessive need to work out.

Charlie shot him a doubtful look. "Maybe you should try Xanax."

"No drugs," Dave pushed back. "I don't need them," he said, defending himself against what he felt were Charlie's hurtful accusations.

"Dave, there's no shame in medication."

Dave gave Charlie a piercing look. The conversation was over.

Charlie regrouped. "Well, I'm glad we took the first flight out. The sun will be coming up soon. We'll have all day to settle in, unpack, and go grocery shopping."

Dave shifted, stretching his arms overhead to ease the tightness in his lower back. "I hope we like living in Phoenix."

"We'll love it. And if it's any consolation, I'm proud of you. Not many men in their fifties would have the courage to take a new job. It's says a lot about you."

"That I'm an idiot," Dave said tongue-in-cheek, as he twisted about his finger the black onyx ring Charlie had given him years earlier.

Charlie shook his head. "No, you have faith in the future," he countered as the plane suddenly shook violently, the thrust so sharp, it caught both men off guard. Dave grabbed Charlie's hand as the yellow oxygen masks dropped, dangling just above their heads.

"Oh my God," Charlie said, his voice dead serious.

"It's just a little thermal inversion," Dave snapped as he slipped the plastic mask over his head, all the while trying to remember to breathe normally.

* * *

Daisy Ellen Lee was a fixture in her Biltmore Greens neighborhood. Spry and energetic, she attributed her vigor to the Phoenix climate. While others complained about the intense summer heat, Daisy likened herself to the mighty saguaro, the desert cactus that dotted the Arizona landscape. During the summer months the saguaro stood tall, defying the searing desert sun. Come the monsoon season, the prickly succulent miraculously budded, yielding an array of bright white flowers. Daisy admired the saguaro's resilience. If the saguaro was a survivor, then so was she.

Each morning, Daisy walked the gated community, part ambassador, part drill sergeant, undertaking the morning inspection of the grounds. She was barely five foot two, even with her blond bouffant teased to a fluffy fullness. Final Net held it perfectly in place. From a distance, in her green lululemon yoga attire, she resembled a yellow poppy on the march.

The exclusive neighborhood of Biltmore Greens abutted the grounds of the Arizona Biltmore Hotel, a five-star resort opened in 1929 and visited by United States presidents, the Hollywood elite, and foreign and national dignitaries. Designed in the architectural style of Frank Lloyd Wright, the Arizona Biltmore, and the developments that encircled the property were a much-desired address in Phoenix.

"Well, good Sunday morning. You're certainly up early," called out Sheila, who worked the midnight shift on the security gate. Her bright red hair was pulled tightly back from her moon-shaped face into a neatly knotted bun that rested at the back of her head just above the neck. The severity of her hairstyle matched her uniform of blue polyester pants and jacket, interrupted by a white cotton button-down shirt.

"I couldn't sleep," Daisy admitted, eyeing the broken concrete block on the base of the little gatehouse.

"Is anything wrong?" Sheila asked.

"When are they fixing that?" Daisy pointed at the offending block. She'd complained about it at the last Homeowner's Association meeting.

"Next Tuesday. I received the notice yesterday."

"Oh, that's good." Daisy gently nudged a loose stone back with her foot into the small rock garden that decorated the side of the gatehouse. "And how's your mother feeling? Is her back any better?"

"She's much better," Sheila answered.

"Oh, I'm so glad," Daisy said, checking the chalkboard on the side of the gatehouse. She didn't expect to see her name on the list of residents who had packages waiting to be picked up, but checking the board was as much a habit as retrieving the mail. She laughed at her own foolishness.

"And how are you feeling this morning?" Sheila asked.

"I awoke with such an unusual burst of energy," Daisy recalled. "So eager to greet all the flowers and shrubs and say hello to my four-legged friends. Silly, isn't it?"

Daisy adored the dogs of the Biltmore. Unlike Sheila, who knew every resident by name and house number, Daisy knew the neighbors through their dogs.

"And who have you seen so far?"

"I saw Jasmine go by with her two Dads. And Millie on her way to Starbucks at Fashion Mall with her folks."

"Lovely," Sheila said as the eastern sky started to brighten. "The sun will be up any minute. It's almost time for the shift change. Bert should be here soon."

Daisy repeated the weather forecast from the morning news. "It's going to be eighty-five with lots of sunshine."

A gentle breeze stirred the smell of orange blossoms. Both women inhaled and sighed.

"Spring is in the air," Daisy wistfully acknowledged. "Ah, another year older come May."

"I just hope when I'm seventy-five," Sheila said, "I look as good as you."

Daisy was pleased to see the admiration in the younger woman's eyes. "Yoga," Daisy declared. "Stretching is the best medicine. I'm going this afternoon to a hot yoga class."

"They have hot yoga for seniors?" Sheila asked in disbelief.

Daisy frowned. "It's not a seniors class," she said. "Why would I be in a seniors class?" It irked her that anyone would make such an assumption.

"Oh," Sheila said, seemingly unaware of her faux pas. "But aren't you uncomfortable . . . can you keep up?"

"Absolutely. And I love young people. All tatted, like walking canvasses. You can learn a lot about them based on their artwork."

Sheila giggled.

Daisy bent down to retie a lace. "When you're young, there's so much to occupy your time. Jobs and school . . . oh these young people come and go . . . in such a rush to get to the *next place*. I'm practically standing still watching as life passes by. It can be a bit lonely."

Sheila looked astonished. "You . . . lonely? I don't believe it. You always seem so active. Going to all those meetings for the Democratic Party. And the Breast Cancer Walks. And gathering signatures on the latest petition drive. My goodness. I don't know where you get the energy."

"Well, I do try to stay engaged and mentally sharp. Oh, but I get lonely. I've lost so many friends over the years. I almost hate to read the obituaries. And those poor souls who wind up in nursing homes . . . that's the worst. I guess life's a crapshoot. You never know how it's going to end."

Unnerved by the conversation's sudden change in tone, Daisy decided to move on.

"Well, dear . . . it was wonderful seeing you . . . you have yourself a glorious day," she said sweetly, waving goodbye.

* * *

Charlie stood with Dave at the luggage carousel at Sky Harbor Airport. He placed his right foot on top of the of conveyor belt, staking out his territory as the other passengers crowded about.

"I can't believe the oxygen mask dropped," Dave said. He shook his head as if reimagining the entire fiasco. "That scared the shit out of me."

"Me too," Charlie admitted. "In all my years of flying, that's never happened."

Dave slipped out of his pullover. The change in climate from the Bay Area to Phoenix was already noticeable. "That last hard bounce must have tripped open the compartment."

"Did you see the look on the stewardess's face?" Charlie laughed, remembering the woman's frantic expression. "I thought she'd have a cow."

"Well, to her credit, she jumped right up and tried to close it."

"But you'd already put on the mask." Charlie roared with laughter, capturing the attention of nearby travelers. "Prepared to go down with the plane," he said, index finger in the air.

"Hey, there's nothing wrong with my reflexes," Dave defended himself, now standing behind Charlie. "In a real emergency, I'd have been breathing. You'd have been starved for oxygen."

"Small consolation. In a real emergency, I'd rather not know what's happening."

"Is that why you didn't put on the mask?"

"I couldn't," Charlie admitted. "My heart stopped."

They both laughed, grateful for the release of nervous energy on what was otherwise a stressful day.

"Well, it's all behind us now." Charlie placed his hands on his hips and gently twisted. "Damn those airplane seats." He spied the electronic board. "It's only 9:15. We did okay on time."

"I hope that flight wasn't a bad omen."

"Oh Dave, knock it off. Nothing good comes from a negative attitude. You know, you always *find what you're looking for*. Stop putting out negative vibes. Phoenix is a terrific place. There's culture, it's young and hip. Lots of bars and restaurants . . . we're going to love it."

Dave hated when Charlie lost his patience. "God, you sound like the freaking Chamber of Commerce."

"You've got to look on the bright side," Charlie lectured.

Dave nodded. "The bright side."

Charlie continued. "You've worked hard. We deserve this. In a month, you'll be comfortable in the new job. In three months, you'll feel like you've lived in Phoenix your whole life. Just give yourself time to adjust."

"I know," Dave answered. "I have to go easy."

"You do that," Charlie said as the luggage carousel came to life, "and I'll grab the bags."

* * *

Daisy pulled up to the Biltmore Greens gate in her red Honda Fit. She rolled down her window and greeted Bert who worked the morning shift.

"Bert, it's so good to see you. How are you feeling?"

Bert stepped out of the little gatehouse. "Much better, Ms. Lee. It's kind of you to ask. The doctor told me it was just a touch of sciatica."

"Oh, I'm so glad you're better," Daisy gushed. "I hear that's very pain-ful. "

"Yes, it most certainly is," Bert answered, rubbing the affected leg.

"Well, it's wonderful to see you back."

"Thank you." Bert blushed. "Where are you heading this morning?"

Daisy's voice perked up. "Sprouts. They're having a big sale on pine-apples. They're usually $3.99. Today, they're 99 cents," she whispered in a conspiring voice.

"That *does* sound like quite a sale."

"Would you like me to bring you back one?" Daisy offered.

"Frankly, Ms. Lee, pineapple makes me gassy. I think I'm better off sticking to protein bars."

Daisy had never had a protein bar. She wondered if she'd like it. "Is there anything you might need while I'm out?"

"You're too kind. Please don't bother about me. I'm just fine," Bert replied.

"Well, I better get going then. I'd hate to get caught in noontime traffic when church lets out."

"You have a few hours for that," Bert chuckled, checking his watch. "It's only ten o'clock now. "There's not a lot of traffic on a Sunday."

"But there's nothing worse than driving when the roads are crowded," Daisy confided. "People tailgate, honk their horn, wave wildly at me. I can see them in the rearview mirror. It's so distracting."

"Maybe you're driving too slowly?"

"Oh no, I'm a terrific driver," Daisy said indignantly. "I'm just cautious. My only problem is finding my car in the parking lot."

Bert frowned. "I had an aunt who got lost in a shopping mall. It was quite an ordeal for the family. She was diagnosed with early onset dementia."

"Oh dear, that's terrible. But it's not my memory that's the problem. It's the other cars. They dwarf my little Fit. Last week, my car was parked between a Ford Super Duty and a Chevy Silverado. My Fit looked like a clown car at the circus."

Bert chuckled. "That can certainly be a problem."

"Well, it was lovely seeing you, Bert. I better get on with the day."

"Enjoy the morning," Bert called.

Daisy stepped on the gas pedal and without yielding at the stop sign, brazenly pulled into the intersection, busy thinking about the best way to select a pineapple, by smell or by the ease in which leaves at the crown release. It was too late for her to stop when she finally became aware of the Allied Van Line truck, thanks to the driver leaning down hard on his horn. The squeal of metallic brakes was unmistakable.

* * *

"What do you think?" Dave asked Charlie as they looked about the furnished rental. The relocation company had arranged for the turnkey apartment with its faded beige carpet, old oak furniture, and white walls sporadically decorated with cheaply framed posters of desert landscapes. Dave thought it horribly ugly.

"It'll have to do," Charlie answered, "though I wish we'd talked before you agreed to this particular apartment."

"Why?" Dave asked. "They assured me every apartment is exactly the same. There's a second bedroom for your office. When they connect the Internet, you'll be all set to work. And it's close to shopping and the freeway. Besides, it's only temporary until you find us a house."

"Yes, but we face west." Charlie tapped on the window that looked out onto the community pool below. "That means intense afternoon sun. And with these cheap, single pane windows, it'll get nice and toasty."

"Oh geez, Charlie, I didn't even think about that." Dave was suddenly aware that the room was already on the warm side. He'd have to find the thermostat and turn on the air.

"Well, it's okay. We're here now." Charlie waved a hand, the sign that he was ready to make the best of it.

"How bad can it get?" Dave wondered, setting the thermostat at sixty-eight, upset that he hadn't asked for Charlie's input before he made the final arrangements.

"May is when the heat really ratchets up to triple digits."

There was a violent rumble above as the air conditioning unit situated on the roof jerked into action. A musty odor filled the room.

"Well that settles it," Dave announced. "We're going to have to be in a new house by May."

"Two months isn't a lot of time to find a place," Charlie warned, flopping down on the tan sofa. The expression on Charlie's face warned Dave that the cushions were hard. Charlie poked at the fake potted fern on the oak coffee table. "Are they kidding with this?" He held up the green plant by one of its floppy plastic leafs. "This thing weighs nothing."

"How hard can it be to find a place?" Dave called out as he opened the cabinets in the tiny galley kitchen, finding the glassware and dishes. "We're sitting on cash from our sale in California. We should be able to find a terrific house." He ran a finger over the white linoleum countertop. They'd need to purchase cleaning supplies. "Remember the homes you showed me in that real estate magazine?"

"Too far from your office," Charlie said, bending the plastic leaf on the fake cactus back and forth.

"But they're all new subdivisions," Dave remembered. Some of the houses appeared palatial.

"That's Chandler and Ahwatuckee," Charlie answered, shaking the coffee table to determine which leg was loose.

"Awaa . . . what?"

"Never mind. The Phoenix metropolitan area is huge. We'll need to find something closer to your office so that you don't spend your drive time in bumper-to-bumper traffic."

"Well, you'll find something." Dave was certain. "I have faith in you." He began loading the cheap ceramic dishes directly from the cabinet into the dishwasher. "When you're done over there," he said to Charlie, who was still playing with the coffee table, "how about stripping the bed? I think we better wash everything before we sleep on it."

Charlie checked his watch. "Okay, it's ten after ten now. I say we spend an hour or so working on this place, unpacking, and then head off to lunch."

Dave nodded. "You got a deal."

* * *

Daisy's forehead rested on a deployed airbag. She felt slightly nauseous from the adrenaline coursing through her body. The truck had slowed, and still, the Honda Fit had taken a hit to the passenger side. Daisy's body had jerked hard against the driver's side door before coming to rest. She'd heard a crack, like stepping on a branch in the forest. The sound had seemed to come from deep within her own body.

"Ma'am, are you okay? Please tell me you're okay." A man with a deep, gruff voice pleaded as he removed his Arizona Diamondbacks ballcap to reveal beads of sweat pouring from his brow. "I'll never forgive myself if you're dead."

"I'm not dead," Daisy finally confessed as she lifted her head, face flushed. "I'll be fine." She looked at the expression on the poor man's face and took pity on him. "I'm just a little stunned."

"Thank God," the man said, wiping his brow with the back of his hand. "You really should pay closer attention," he now scolded her. "When was the last time someone gave you a driving test? Jesus. You gave me the scare of a lifetime."

"Ms. Lee, are you okay?" Bert called, running up to the site of the collision, cell phone in hand, the 911 operator still on the line.

"She's fine," the truck driver answered, eyeing the damage to the car. "She's absolutely fine."

"Now you stay still," Bert advised. "The ambulance should be here any minute."

Daisy could hear the approach of emergency sirens. "Oh Bert," she softly said, "I don't need an ambulance." But when she tried to move, there was a gnawing pain in her left hip. She winced as the ache intensified.

"Now please, Ms. Lee. Don't move," Bert instructed as the first EMT approached. "I'm here with you. Don't you worry."

Daisy felt flush. "Oh Bert" were the last words she managed before everything went black.

* * *

Phoenix's well-trained EMTs surrounded the vehicle as Daisy came to. On a scale of one to ten, the pain was fifteen. Daisy cried out in agony as she was lifted from the car and placed on a stretcher. Any movement was sheer torture. The sharp, stabbing sensation in her left hip ruled every breath.

The ambulance ride was a blur.

At the hospital, a young emergency room physician, with blond wavy hair and an angelic smile, provided morphine. Daisy sighed as the drug, injected directly into her IV, immediately took effect. "Thank you," she said, her heart full of gratitude as the pain finally receded.

"While you rest," the doctor quietly advised, "we're going to schedule that hip for surgery."

"Oh dear," was all Daisy could muster. *Surgery is such serious business,* she thought, focusing her attention on the doctor's mouth, watching and waiting for his lips to once again move.

The doctor scanned Daisy's chart as he engaged her in light conversation "The paramedics said you were lucky. Your age . . . the nature of the accident . . . you could have been seriously hurt."

His comment rubbed her the wrong way. Adrenaline surged through her small frame and perhaps due to the morphine, she spoke sharply before thinking. "This isn't serious enough?"

The doctor pulled up a chair and sat beside her bed. "Ms. Lee, your broken hip was not a result of an auto accident," the doctor explained. "We see this all the time. A woman who presents as perfectly healthy suddenly falls to the ground. She thinks she's tripped. She hasn't. It's osteoporosis. The disease generates weak bones and in women of a certain age, fragile hips. You broke that hip in a seated position. It was primed to break."

Daisy could hardly believe her ears. She'd heard of osteoporosis, but she'd always thought such a condition was evidenced by poor posture. She hadn't realized that someone who stood perfectly straight could experience the effects in places other than the spine.

"It could have happened in the supermarket or in the privacy of your bathroom. You were lucky. There were people around. Have you spoken with your primary care physician about osteoporosis?" His warm blue eyes pressed her for an answer.

She folded her hands in her lap, fingers intertwined, like a schoolgirl, politely waiting for the teacher to reveal the day's lesson. "No," Daisy admitted. "I don't have a primary care doctor."

The young physician was unable to hide his surprise. His response was quick and abrupt. "And why is that?"

Daisy hesitated. She wondered if it might be rude to share her theory about doctors with a doctor. She'd always been a confident woman, and yet here, in this antiseptic environment, with everyone dressed in white coats and green scrubs, clearly knowledgeable about things she only guessed at, she reconsidered her opinions.

The young physician awaited her response.

She cleared her throat and lifted her chin slightly, believing a regal posture lent authority to her words. "I think doctors overmedicate seniors. For every complaint, they write a prescription. I don't believe in drugs. I don't think they're good for you. I think they bring on confusion in people my age." She paused and took a deep breath before continuing. "There's nothing in my medicine cabinet besides lipstick and face powder," she proudly boasted. "I've been healthy all my life. Why would I pay a doctor to search for problems where none exist?"

The doctor glared at her. She cringed. She'd angered him.

"Do you realize the risk you're taking? Osteoporosis is a serious condition that should be managed. And at your age, you need a family physician. I hope you've at least had an annual flu shot."

Daisy blushed. She'd passed on flu shots. What was the point? She never got sick.

The young doctor shook his head. He returned to the discussion at hand. "The orthopedic surgeon will stop by later. A counselor will also come by and make sure your paperwork is in order, including emergency contacts."

"Emergency contacts?" Daisy repeated.

"Ms. Lee, you're having surgery. It's a serious matter. We need to know who to talk with in case there's a problem."

"Oh my," Daisy fretted. "I really don't have anyone. My family is back east and we've lost touch."

"No children?"

"No," Daisy confirmed.

"Friends. You have friends?"

"Well, I did, but . . ." and Daisy stammered unable to complete the sentence. She was suddenly very tired.

The doctor bit his lower lip. Daisy wondered if he'd encountered her situation before. An older person admitted to the ER with no available next of kin. How many other seemingly alert, independent seniors found themselves alone during a health crisis?

He stood up. "Okay then. We'll have a social worker stop by. Don't worry about it," he said, leaning over and squeezing her hand.

It was a kind gesture. Daisy appreciated the change in his manner. If only she could remember his name. He must have told her, but then it seemed rude to ask again. Instead, she accepted his warmth and was grateful. Whatever his name, at least there was a heart behind that tough clinical exterior.

* * *

"Isn't this nice?" Charlie said, taking a deep breath and enjoying the fresh air. "We're sitting outside and eating lunch. The sun is shining, the sky is blue. It's not too warm. You can even see Camelback Mountain from here. It's Shangri-La."

The hour in the apartment had made Dave tense; now Charlie was trying to get him to relax, but it was difficult.

Dave nodded grudgingly. "It *is* wonderful."

"And after we eat and go to the grocery store, maybe we'll take a nap." Charlie lifted an eyebrow provocatively.

"We'll see," Dave answered. He looked down at the brunch menu. "Do you know what you're having? What looks good?"

"I think *I do*," Charlie said, his voice throaty. He leaned forward and winked.

"Okay, okay, I get it, Mr. Subtle," Dave answered. "How about we order before we make plans for the rest of the day?"

"Sex will relax you," Charlie coaxed.

"Don't feel like it," Dave said. "Not when I'm upset."

Charlie placed his menu on the table. "A little backrub and you'll be fine."

But Dave was not to be persuaded. "It's best to leave me alone when I'm in a mood."

Charlie said nothing.

"Did you hear me?" Dave asked.

"Okay . . . okay . . . I hear you," Charlie acknowledged. "Just trying to help."

A tow truck passed by. A red Honda Fit was hoisted high in the air, the passenger side punched in. Charlie nodded in the truck's direction. "Check that out. Someone's really having a bad day." Dave turned to see the damaged vehicle. "See . . . we have everything going for us," Charlie continued. "You've got a new job. We're healthy. The weather is terrific. We're so lucky."

Dave nodded, hesitantly.

"We have a great life," Charlie continued.

Dave had to agree.

"You should be more mindful of that," Charlie counseled. "And appreciative, instead of getting yourself all worked up and stressed out. A wrecked car . . . that's a problem."

Dave's appetite improved. "Okay, I'm going to get the Greek salad with chicken," he said, more positively. "That sounds good. And an order of hummus. We can split it."

"Okay." Charlie brightened. He waited for Dave to put his menu down before signaling for the waitress.

"And maybe I'll have a Diet Coke," Dave added.

"How about just water?" Charlie suggested. "We're in the desert. You should be drinking plenty of water," he said, knowing from experience that carbonation and sex didn't mix.

"Okay," Dave acquiesced.

Charlie assumed a Cheshire smile as the waitress approached. *Putty in my hands*, he thought. *He's just putty in my hands.*

2

·····························

When Daisy awoke, she had no idea whether it was day or night. A bright white curtain created a makeshift space that separated her from the rest of the world. Beside her, an electronic monitor seemed to repeatedly hum, *hello there hello there hello there.*

She felt small, fragile, and very alone.

She inhaled and exhaled in a series of slow, deep breaths. She'd learned in yoga about the importance of the breath to ease anxiety, but now, she was unable to achieve any sense of calm. She was too scared about what might happen next.

Tears came to her eyes as her mind drifted back to the day when she'd begun her journey to this place in the desert.

It was August 12, 1952.

She was eighteen years old, standing on the platform at Grand Central Station in an inexpensive blue traveling suit and matching navy beret, white gloves, and holding a straw purse, all purchased from Gimbel's bargain basement. She'd wanted to go to California but could barely afford the fare to Phoenix. With both parents long gone, she was on her own. Still, it had been a heart-wrenching decision to leave New York City. She adored her older brother Jacob, but her sister-in-law Rose had made it clear that Daisy had to leave.

How different my life would have been if I hadn't . . .

The thought stopped midstream. Buried pain was best left in the past. And yet she couldn't resist a final memory. The beautiful eyes searching her face; tiny hands peeking out from a blue blanket; the smell of talcum powder on his warm, little body.

She held her breath as she remembered.

When Daisy arrived in Phoenix, America was in the midst of a post-war industrial boom. Jobs were plentiful. Phoenix was a sleepy town of mostly one-story buildings. Outside the city perimeter, it was still cowboy country—sunburned men with hats and chaps, horses, corrals, and trails across the desert. Daisy landed her first job as a barmaid at the San Carlos Hotel. For most women of her generation, marriage came before work, and yet marriage eluded her. Men came and went, none staying too long. Daisy adjusted. She bore her disappointments quietly. Life taught her that nothing was guaranteed. If she wanted to survive, she'd have to learn to take care of herself. She'd have to be strong. It had been a hard lesson.

A nurse appeared from behind the curtain.

"Ms. Lee, we're just about ready. How are you doing?"

Daisy was too upset to answer and tried, instead, to smile. The young woman stroked Daisy's arm as she checked the IV, then slipped a pair of socks on her feet. The pain from her hip was gone. The nurse pushed aside the curtain and maneuvered the gurney down a short hallway and into a room with a bright white light. A drug was administered as she was instructed to count backward from ten. Somewhere between nine and eight Daisy found a peaceful freedom from thought . . . a total immersion into the unconscious.

* * *

Dave stifled a yawn. He'd arrived at 7:30 a.m. for his first day on the new job. After grabbing a glazed donut and a cup of coffee, he found an aisle seat in the crowded auditorium where new hires from across the regional market were going through a communal orientation. At the front of the room, there was a large screen. Projected in large white letters against a dark-blue background . . . *The Mission of Bremer Health*. On the stage, a young woman in her late twenties, a manager in human resources, repeatedly checked her watch as Dave took the first bite of his donut. *Dear God*, he thought, savoring the sugary goodness. *When was the last time I had a donut?* He licked his lips and sipped the coffee; the combination, pure pleasure.

As the other new hires settled into their seats, Dave spotted Phyllis, his boss's secretary, entering the front of the auditorium through a side door marked *Exit*. It had been weeks since they'd last seen each other at his final interview. She scanned the auditorium, eyeglasses perched atop her luxurious blond mane, wearing a blue knit dress that seemed a bit too tight for her curvaceous figure. Phyllis appeared stressed as she looked about. Dave wondered what could possibly be wrong. He stifled a second yawn as Phyllis slipped on her eyeglasses, squinted, and then nodded in his direction. She hurried over. "Mr. Greenway?" she asked, kneeling next to his chair.

"Yes," he answered, suddenly aware she wasn't quite sure. Up close, he could see the dark circles gathered under her lovely eyes. He guessed she was in her late thirties.

"I'm so sorry," she said, "but it's been crazy around here. I just processed four job offers last week for new executives. I'm having trouble keeping the names and faces straight."

Dave smiled. That seemed like a lot of new positions. He hoped Bremer was expanding. More jobs, more opportunity.

"Mr. Allman wants you to join the executive team meeting," she said. "You'd better bring your things along. These meetings can run long."

Dave grabbed his briefcase and followed Phyllis out of the auditorium, struggling to keep up as she rushed down the hallway toward the executive boardroom.

"Every Monday morning the executive team meets," she called back to him, miraculously balancing the shifting weight of her ample backside on a pair of six-inch black heels. "The meeting will always be on your calendar for 8:00 a.m. and Mr. Allman expects everyone to be prompt." She touched the knob to the boardroom and then stepped back, nodding to Dave to open the door and go inside.

All eyes turned as Dave entered. He was motioned to a chair at the end of a large conference table. Daniel Allman, Chief Operating Officer of Bremer Health, sat at the head. Daniel made the brief introduction. "Ladies and Gentleman, this is Dave Greenway, our newest vice president."

Heads bobbed and turned. Dave recognized a few of the faces from the organizational chart which had arrived with his relocation packet. The seats at the conference table were filled by hospital CEOs and their medical and nursing leadership. Lesser executives, directors and managers, sat in chairs scattered about the room. Dave had never seen so much high-priced talent gathered in one place for a weekly meeting. He'd researched the market and knew many of the executives had journeyed for hours to be in attendance.

Daniel returned the group's focus to the agenda. As Daniel spoke about financial targets, Dave remembered the first time they'd met. He'd been impressed by Daniel's sheer size. He stood six foot four with the build of a retired basketball player who had filled out after a few years off the court. His huge mitts clasped Dave's hand with an energy that had caught Dave totally off guard.

"I'll be frank," Daniel had said, "I need your expertise to help run this place. Sometimes, I think I'm surrounded by idiots. Right now the corporate office is all over my tail. But I don't give a rat's ass about them. Only the Chairman of the Board has the power to hire and fire me. The corporate office is just so much background noise."

Dave had been charmed by Daniel. He appreciated his honesty. He appreciated his informal manner. But now, Dave wondered how Daniel ran his empire, as he refocused back on the meeting.

"I'm going to ask again," Daniel said, glancing about the room, "who shared this month's financials with the corporate office?"

The tension in the room was palpable as Dave coyly looked about, trying to put faces together with the photos and bios he'd been given. He'd have to know the players if he expected to hit the floor running.

Craig De Coy was the first to speak.

Dave recognized Craig from his brush cut. He was a first-time CEO who had held lesser positions in small, rural, community hospitals.

Craig leaned forward, breaking the line of straight-backed executives who had turned to face Daniel. "Corporate tells us to send the information directly to them. What else can we do?"

"You call me," Daniel said sharply. "I've told you that I'll handle all communications with corporate."

"But they leave us no option," Craig insisted. "They expect immediate turnaround."

"That's ridiculous," Daniel said, his voice booming. "How many times are we going to have this conversation? How many times do I have to repeat myself?"

Daniel looked about as if he actually expected someone to answer the question. There was total silence.

He continued. "If the people in this room are unable to put off corporate, maybe you shouldn't be in the C-suite."

"That's not fair," Craig responded, his face bright red, sounding like a third-grader objecting to a homework assignment.

Daniel scanned the room. His dark eyes defying anyone to speak. "Who else doesn't think it's fair?"

Barely a breath was taken.

"It appears you're alone in that opinion, Craig. Perhaps if you ran your operation as well as you answer to corporate, you'd have hit your budget targets this month."

Craig clenched his jaw. The muscles in his cheeks visibly flexed. Dave wondered how long Craig planned to stay in his job. His future with the company seemed bleak.

Daniel's tone shifted. "How do you think I feel when corporate asks me to explain financials I haven't yet seen? All they want to do is catch me off-guard. Make me sweat." He was now playing the martyr. "Those people don't know how to run a business. They're bean counters. I'm the one holding this ship together. So remember, the next time the corporate office calls, it's the regional office that pays your salary. You do what I tell you," he insisted. "I hired you, and by God, I'll fire you! Is everybody clear on that?"

Dave couldn't believe his ears. Is this how the company conducted its meetings? Like an over-the-top Telemundo drama?

Daniel next held up a packet of handouts. Colored pie charts graphed each hospital's performance according to Medicare's quality standards. Green indicated success; yellow, the need for improvement. Nearly every page was dominated by red.

Daniel focused on Craig. "Your hospital's performance is especially dismal," he bristled.

Craig glanced at his chief nursing officer. A middle-aged, attractive brunette, nervously recounted the steps that the hospital was taking to turn the subpar performance. Dave watched Daniel's face as he listened to the woman. It was quiet, impassive. After three minutes had passed, Daniel suddenly pounded the conference table with a closed fist. The force was so great, that the modem at the center leapt from its position. "Bullshit," Daniel shouted. "This is all bullshit."

The poor woman sat slack-jawed, unable to continue.

Daniel stood up. He held the offending data above his head and glared about the room, like an angry giant reaching for the heavens. "I've had it with these excuses, people. Get ready to change jobs because I won't tolerate this kind of performance."

Executives shifted nervously in their chairs as Daniel headed to the door. Before leaving, he slammed the offending packet into the waste can with such force, that it crashed loudly onto its side and rolled over. The sound, a veritable bomb going off, reverberated throughout the room.

After Daniel's exit, the people in the room gathered up their belongings. Empty pads slid into cases, and unused pens dropped into satchels. One-by-one they rose. Defeated children.

Dave's heart sank. *Bullying to achieve results. What have I done? This isn't the work environment I signed up for.*

"Buck up," Charlie said later that evening. "It was probably a once-in-a-blue-moon meeting. Executives don't behave like that."

"I don't know," Dave said. "There was so much negative energy."

"Dave, you're exaggerating."

"I wish I was. I just hope he doesn't go off on me."

"He won't," Charlie insisted. "You're the fair-haired child. He paid a lot of money to recruit you."

"Something tells me he takes no prisoners," Dave worried. "This guy doesn't play well with others."

* * *

While Daisy's surgeon described the operation as a success, she wasn't quite so sure. The total hip replacement had left her in severe pain, and for the first time in Daisy's life, she welcomed medication. Lots of medication. So much medication, she lost the ability to stay in the moment. One day blended into the next. People came in and out of her hospital room. If strangers introduced themselves, Daisy was too groggy to remember who they were or why they were there.

The nurses insisted Daisy get up and walk. That was the first rule following surgery. She tried. But despite the objections of the nursing staff, the pain from the incision and the dizziness from all the medication forced her back to bed. She wanted to rest. She had to rest.

But resting in a hospital is impossible.

Daisy lingered the maximum number of days allowed by Medicare before a young woman in a white coat visited. She told Daisy arrangements had been made to transfer her to a rehabilitation facility. Daisy couldn't remember the details of the conversation, how the decision was made, or who actually made it, but there was no turning back. The young woman toting the documents had made that very clear. They needed to free up the bed.

Luis, a nurse's aide, showed up the next morning.

A large Hispanic man with a sweet disposition, Luis helped Daisy to sit up. "Pardon me," he said, slipping his huge hands under Daisy's armpits, before pulling her close. She could smell his Paco Rabanne. He gently lifted her, and in one smooth motion, shifted her into the wheelchair he'd placed bedside.

The soreness in her hip was a potent clarifier of the day's activities. It effectively cut through the confusion of the pain medication. She was once again alert to her surroundings.

Luis glided the wheelchair down the hallway, past the nurse's station, to the elevators flanked by floor-to-ceiling mirrors. Daisy couldn't imagine why anyone would install mirrors in a hospital. She caught sight of her reflection. She flinched. She had no makeup on. Her bouffant hairdo looked like a deflated balloon. She'd planned to have her ash-blond color touched up before the accident, but had missed the appointment. Dark grey roots created a two-tone effect.

I look like a psychiatric patient who just had electroshock therapy, she thought sadly.

The elevator doors opened. It was midday and the car was crowded. Strangers stared at her. She took a deep breath and resigned herself to the situation. She didn't look her best and there was absolutely nothing she could do about it. She was at the mercy of her left hip.

A young man with shaggy brown hair wearing a *Jesus Loves Me* tee shirt smiled politely and stepped to the side of the elevator. Luis turned the wheelchair around and pulled Daisy in backward. There was just enough room.

Daisy faced the front of the car. In the reflection of the metallic doors, she could see a girl of six or seven standing nearby, cradling a stuffed floppy-eared white bunny in her arms, sneaking furtive glances at a bald spot on the side of Daisy's head. The child's eyes searched Daisy's crown like an explorer traveling through uncharted waters. Daisy closed her eyes to block the little girl out.

When the elevator doors opened onto the lobby, a stiff breeze blew up from the shaft. The gust caught Daisy by surprise. She struggled to keep the front of the flimsy green hospital gown closed but her fingers were like hardened rubber. The two tiny strings, barely knotted in a bow, unraveled. As the wheelchair advanced, the gown slipped hopelessly out of Daisy's grasp and caught in the mechanism of the wheel. Kindly strangers turned away. Others stared as she fumbled and tugged on the trapped gown, bare breasts exposed.

Daisy blushed crimson.

Luis pulled the chair backward in an effort to release the gown as he reached over Daisy's head to stop the elevator door from bouncing back and forth against the wheelchair. The first bounce had created a high-pitched beeping which had alerted security. Daisy was soon surrounded by uniformed guards.

Luis successfully freed the gown, but the damage had been done. The child who stood at Daisy's side had witnessed the entire debacle. The mother tugged roughly on the little girl's hand before she finally left the elevator.

What had taken less than three minutes to unfold felt as if it had happened in slow motion.

Daisy boldly returned the gaze of those in the lobby who'd been too shocked to look away. She nodded politely, as if it had all been planned. She pretended she was enjoying a ride in an Audi convertible on a warm Phoenix day. And though nothing could have been further from the truth, for that moment, Daisy shifted reality.

"Daisy Ellen Lee?" asked the driver, an African-American man whose bent posture and graying hair hinted he was well past retirement age. He took the paperwork from Luis and quickly compared it to his own documents. "Yup, that's you," the man answered with a warm smile. "You just sit tight and relax."

The wheelchair was rolled onto the van's electronic hoist. In moments, Daisy was lifted like so much cargo. "There you go," the driver said, unlocking the safety and pushing the wheelchair into place, his brown eyes projecting pure kindness and consideration. With a quick snap, he locked the chair. "Now that wasn't so bad."

The hospital disappeared in the distance. Daisy thought, *Thank God, I'll never see those people again* as she tightened her grip on the hospital gown, reliving the experience.

"I'll have you at The Village in no time," the driver called back.

Along the interior walls of the van were large glossy photographs of active seniors. A fashionably dressed woman, silver hair cut in a short perky bob, gaily held a glass of red wine, smiling as if ready to make a toast; a handsome gentleman in a bright green Tommy Hilfiger golf shirt and white shorts was on the greens, club in hand, preparing to putt; an older woman emerged from a hot tub, cap adorned in brightly colored flowers, her smile beaming. The Village promised to offer more than rehabilitation. It professed to be a lifestyle community.

Daisy thought, *The Village . . . now that's a lovely name.*

* * *

Jack Lee broke into a big grin as his 2007 white Ford Escape passed Anthem on Interstate 17 heading south. He'd spotted the olive green marker. *Phoenix – 33 miles.* They'd traveled three days, stopping overnight in St. Louis and Amarillo, some two thousand miles across country from Detroit. Enid, his wife, fast asleep in the passenger seat, was gently snoring. She'd drifted off somewhere south of Flagstaff, leaving Jack alone to thrill at the majesty of the red rocks of Sedona.

Growing up in New York, Jack had often heard about Arizona from his father Jacob who had boasted of having a sister, an aunt Jack had never met, who'd settled in the Phoenix area. Cowboys. Desert. Wide open spaces. Jack fondly remembered his father expressing an interest in visiting, though he never did get west of the Mississippi. Together, they watched *Wagon Train*, *Bonanza*, and *Have Gun—Will Travel*. Jack could never seem to get enough of the Westerns. And then, in 1985, Jack made his first trip to Phoenix to attend a conference at the Arizona Biltmore. The memory of the beautiful property and the surrounding homes had stayed with him. *I'm going to live here someday*, he thought.

It was a promise he'd been determined to keep.

"Hey, sleepyhead," he said, gently nudging his wife's shoulder, "you've got to see this. The scenery is amazing."

Enid, a petite woman of delicate features, who wore her dark auburn hair in a severe mannish cut, opened her eyes. "My God, it's so bright," she said, shielding her face with her hand. "Someone dim the lights."

"You're just tired. It's been a long trip. But I promise, you're going to love it."

"You didn't tell me you could go blind from the sun." She pulled down the car visor.

"We'll get you a pair of dark shades. Heck, we'll be like movie stars and tint the car windows. '*Who's that?*' everyone will ask. '*Enid and Jack Lee. They're new here.*'"

Enid shifted in her seat. "Are you being funny, Jack?" she said with a withering glance.

"Come on. This is the beginning of a new life. Arizona. Yee ha!"

"Jack," she admonished him, checking her hair in the visor mirror, "you're acting like John Wayne is going to show up atop a stagecoach with guns blazing. Phoenix is a sophisticated city. Last night when you drifted off, I read *Fodor's*. The days of the Wild West are over," she announced with certainty.

"Ah, but nature is everywhere. Just look around. You can see it in the cacti and the desert landscapes. So beautiful. This is a dream come true for me." His voice was barely able to contain his excitement.

Enid sighed. "I don't know why I let you talk me into this. Why not Florida? What was wrong with Boca Raton? I have family there."

"Enid, this is an adventure." Jack sidestepped the perilous trap of commenting on Enid's family. "We can still vacation in Boca."

Enid nodded, seemingly appeased.

Jack caught sight of an eagle soaring overhead. His heart skipped a beat. *Besides*, he thought about Florida, *if I wanted to live in a damp swamp, I'd have moved to the bayous of Louisiana.*

* * *

Jack Lee couldn't wait to get out of Michigan. After thirty years teaching high school history in Detroit, he was terrified that his pension might be affected by the trials and tribulations of Michigan's financial woes. The auto industry was on its knees, with the city of Detroit struggling to find bottom. Sick of listening to the daily drumbeat of financial mismanagement, he and Enid had agreed to sell their historic Indian Village home after the fourth break-in in two years. Each time, they'd been lucky. Neither of them had been home. The following week Jack was on a plane to Phoenix where he made an offer on a two-bedroom townhouse in The Biltmore Terraces; a great property with views of the golf course.

"It's so small, Jack," Enid complained when she reviewed the property online.

Jack was not about to be second-guessed. "We're awfully lucky to have picked up a Biltmore property at such a great price. And this is the time in life when we can do with a little less. Besides, that house perfectly fits our budget."

Another reason Jack had pressed for Arizona was its reasonable cost of living. Too young for social security, he'd seen the value of Enid's trust setup by her father, tumble. Over the years, it had generated enough income to keep Enid in the style she craved. But with the uncertainty of the times, and the bottoming of the stock market, the value of the portfolio was at an all-time low. They'd have to watch their spending.

"It won't be long now," Jack said as the car headed down Missouri Avenue toward 24th Street. "Look at those hedges."

A high wall of greenery enshrined the one-square-mile Biltmore property that included the hotel and surrounding property.

"Oh my God," Enid gasped, her mood suddenly brightening. "You didn't tell me it was so private and lush. It's as lovely as the Boca Raton Hotel and Country Club."

They crossed 24th Street and entered the Biltmore. Enid sat up straight and adjusted her blouse. Jack smiled as she checked her face in the mirror.

"Where's my lipstick?" She searched her bag. "Jack, you didn't tell me it was so exclusive. I should have worn something nicer."

Enid's eyes popped as the car crossed the 18-hole golf course before passing the many mansions that lined Thunderbird Drive. Jack was thrilled that she was so excited. *I knew she'd love it. She just needed to experience it.* A quick right, and the car stopped at the gate of the Biltmore Terraces.

"Hello," Jack said to the redhead who popped her head out of the window to greet him. "We're the Lees. We're new. You should be expecting us."

The woman checked the roster. "Lee, Lee. Oh yes. Here you are. Well, welcome. I'm Sheila. I'm filling in today, but anything you need, be sure to ask."

"So you're new too," Jack said exuberantly.

Enid nudged him with her elbow. It was her cue for him to stop talking to strangers.

"Not exactly," Sheila explained. "I work full-time at Biltmore Greens. I'm just helping out today." She handed Jack a manila envelope. "Inside is a parking pass and a decal for your window. Make sure you place the sticker on the inside driver's side. It allows you access to all the Biltmore neighborhoods."

"Thank you," Jack beamed. "Tell me, is it always this beautiful here?"

"Absolutely," Sheila smiled.

"This is just a dream come true. A dream come true," he said.

Enid's elbow poked him again.

"I know this is an odd question," Sheila suddenly asked, "but are you folks related to Daisy Ellen Lee?

Jack was astonished. "My father had a sister Daisy who moved to Phoenix. I was just thinking about her."

"There must be a million women named *Daisy* in the world," Enid offered. Her tone left no doubt that she was eager to get past the gate.

"But you did say Daisy Ellen?" Jack clarified with Sheila. "How many *Daisy Ellens* can there be?"

"A quarter of a million," Enid snapped. "At least as many as there are Jack Allen Lees."

"She's a lovely woman," Sheila went on. "Now my brother's daughter, my niece Alison, is the spitting image of me as a girl. Every time I look at her, it's like looking in a mirror. You know, Mr. Lee? The more I look at you, the more I think you and Ms. Lee are just like two peas in a pod. You have the same eyes. It's quite unnerving."

"I wonder if she's my aunt," Jack said to Enid, before turning back to Sheila. "Now that would be quite a coincidence. Tell me, which is Daisy's house? I'd love to meet her."

Sheila's expression shifted. "Oh, I'm sorry," she said, a worried look crossing her face. "Perhaps I shouldn't have said anything. I'm not allowed to provide personal information about the residents. But I'll tell you what. Why don't you give me a note with your name and phone number, and I'll make sure Ms. Lee gets it."

"Fine," Jack agreed. "Whatever works." He waited for Sheila to open the gate. "Imagine that," he said, turning to Enid, "I may have an aunt who lives in the Biltmore. A long-lost aunt. Who'd have guessed?"

* * *

Dear Ms. Lee,

My name is Jack. My wife and I have recently moved to Phoenix. I wonder if we are related. My parents were Jacob and Rose. They're gone now, but I remember my Dad telling me about a sister who lived in Phoenix. Is it possible you're my aunt? If so, we'd love to meet you. Please ask Sheila to share with us your phone number. Or, if you'd like to call us directly, I've enclosed my phone number on the back of this note with our address.

Fondly, Jack Lee

* * *

Later that day, Sheila visited Daisy at The Village. She offered a friendly hello to a gentleman sitting in the lobby before realizing he was babbling to himself. She averted her eyes as she passed the white-haired seniors, dressed in their bedclothes, who lined the hallways slumped over in their wheelchairs, fast asleep. The closer she got to the wing where Daisy was housed, the stronger the smell of urine.

She gagged.

Arriving at Daisy's closed door, she knocked. "Ms. Lee," she called out. "Ms. Lee, are you there?"

There was no response.

She knocked again, this time louder, cracking open the door and peeking inside. The room was dark. It was midafternoon and the Venetian blinds were tightly drawn.

Perhaps this is the wrong room, she thought, rechecking the name on the door. No, she was in the right place.

She entered, slowly approaching Daisy's bedside.

Daisy stirred. A weak voice pleaded, "Nurse, I need to go to the bathroom. Please help me."

"Ms. Lee, it's me, Sheila."

Daisy struggled to focus. "Sheila, where did you come from?"

"I've been concerned about you," Sheila said in a sudden pang of guilt. Why hadn't she made it her business to visit sooner? "How are you?" she asked, helping Daisy to sit up.

"Not well, I'm afraid. I've developed an infection and I have a fever."

Sheila's heart sank.

"They're giving me antibiotics."

"That sounds like the right course."

"I don't know." Daisy shook her head. "I'm so tired . . . and I have terrible cramps. What time is it?"

Sheila looked at the wall clock. "It's three."

"How long have I been here?" Daisy asked.

Sheila had no clue.

"How about we open these blinds?" she suggested, tugging on the little white cord. Light flooded the room. "There, that's better," she said, turning back to Daisy. "It's such a lovely day . . ." she began, as her breath caught in her throat. Seeing Daisy in the bright light, she struggled to suppress her shock. Daisy's face looked haggard. The gentle lines which had once graced her friendly eyes and mouth had deepened severely from sudden weight loss. Her skin was white and pasty, a far cry from Daisy's normal rosy complexion. Daisy was no longer the vital, energetic person Sheila knew. She'd become a withered old woman,

"I wish I felt better," Daisy said, adjusting herself in the bed. "But it is so good of you to visit. How kind."

Sheila leaned against the windowsill, unwilling to commit to a seat. The smell of disinfectant permeated the air. She maintained a pleasant, outward demeanor, all the while knowing that something horrible had happened.

"Bert sends his regards," she said in a chipper voice. "We both came to the hospital to visit but you were really out of it. I'm not sure you even knew we were there."

"I don't remember," Daisy confirmed. "Morphine is an amazing drug."

And then Daisy pulled back the top cover of her bedding. Her feet were blueish-red and swollen. Sheila diverted her eyes, fighting the urge to flee. Instead, she retrieved Jack's note from her purse.

"Well, you'll never guess who I met," she bravely said, holding up the note from Jack which after all had been the reason for her visit. "It was the strangest thing . . ." and as she started to tell the story, a young African-American woman sporting a close-cropped Afro appeared in the doorway.

"Honey," the aide called to Daisy, "have you been ringing for me?"

"Oh yes," Daisy answered, relief in her voice. "I have to go to the bathroom."

Sheila, grateful for the interruption, placed the unopened note on the bedside table. "Well, I better be going," she said, concerned her presence might cause Daisy embarrassment. "I need to get home," she lied, eager to escape. "I just wanted to be sure and bring this note."

Mission accomplished, Sheila was out of the room before the aide lowered the bars on Daisy's bed. She moved quickly down the hallway, past those who seemed frozen in time. *Is this what becomes of us?* Sheila thought, rushing to her car. *I'd rather die than wind up in a place like that.*

* * *

"I'm home," Dave called from the open door, his key still buried in the lock.

He was exasperated. He'd hoped to leave the office early, but cornered at five o'clock, he'd fidgeted his way through an impromptu meeting with Daniel that lasted nearly two hours.

Doesn't he have a wife and a home to go to?

He chalked it up to Daniel's endless need to micromanage.

Charlie stood in the galley kitchen, separated from the living room by an eat-in counter. A small dinette table was within steps. "The roast's in the oven, warming." Charlie came around the counter. "Let me give you a hand with that key. You have to jiggle it."

Dave and Charlie switched positions.

Dave dropped his workbag by the door and headed to the kitchen. "It smells good," he said, spotting the mail on the counter. He looked through the stack.

Charlie twisted and turned, eventually loosening Dave's key before dropping it on the counter. "Hey you," he said approaching Dave from behind. With his arms about Dave's waist, he pulled him in for a hug.

Dave turned, and they kissed. He relaxed into it. It felt damn good. "Sorry about being so late," he apologized. "It's impossible to get out of that building at a reasonable hour. I think this might be the way of life at Bremer."

"I'm just glad you're here. Time to relax."

Dave loosened his tie as Charlie pulled out the roast and placed it on top of the stove.

"So how'd it go today? Any better?" Charlie asked, lifting the roast out of the pan with a large fork to settle it on the carving board.

"Any better than what? The same people, the same meetings, the same Daniel. He has all these questions about the financial performance of the business, which is surprising considering he signed all these terrible contracts. Every lousy deal has his fingerprints on it. And he's so damn angry. He's just a very hostile guy."

Dave spotted an oversized card in the middle of the stack of mail. He opened it. A photograph of two Golden Labs, eyes bright, tongues dangling, smiling the way only Golden Labs seemed to do, stared back at him.

"Well, I have a surprise for you." Charlie pointed at the dining room table, carving knife in hand.

There, sitting on Dave's plate, was a box wrapped with a red bow.

"Oh no," Dave moaned, realizing the card he held had been sent by friends in California. "It's our anniversary . . ."

Charlie smiled. "You make it sound like a terrible thing."

"But I didn't get you anything," Dave said mournfully. "All those early morning meetings and late nights, I kept thinking, *I have to get Charlie a gift*. But I kept running out of time. And then I forgot."

Charlie leaned forward on the counter. "Don't worry about it. You'll take me to dinner this weekend. No big deal."

"Oh Charlie, that isn't right. I wanted you to have something special."

"I *do* have something special." Charlie wiped his hands with a dish towel before pulling Dave into his arms. "I have you. And now, I have Phoenix. Dave, I love it here. This is the best decision we've ever made."

Dave was sorry to hear Charlie say that.

Charlie returned to the galley kitchen. "I couldn't imagine us living anywhere else. I mean, can you believe this weather? In April? It's amazing."

Dave fingered the ribbon on the gift. "I've been thinking this move was a mistake," he said, his voice low, nearly imperceptible. Uncertain Charlie had heard him, he blurted out, "I really can't stand working at Bremer."

Charlie, his back turned to Dave, opened the refrigerator, though he seemed to hear every word. "You just need time to adjust. You'll see. We'll buy a great house, make new friends, and get a dog. We'll have a wonderful life."

"Charlie, I don't know." Dave was heartsick. It had been a long time since he and Charlie had been so far apart on an issue.

Charlie dressed the salad. "You've always been slow to adjust to change. Every new job has been a crisis. Given time, things will smooth over. You'll see. It'll all work out. It's just bumpy in the beginning."

Dave sighed. "I wish I was as optimistic as you."

"Well, you never *have* been," Charlie said. "That word isn't in your vocabulary. You're a worrier."

"But this time it's different," Dave confessed, a hand resting on what remained of the unopened mail, eyes pleading for Charlie to understand. "This is really bad."

"You're upset," Charlie acknowledged. "You've had a hard day. Why don't you go ahead and open your gift."

Dave tore at the paper. *How*, he thought, *can I possibly make Charlie understand?*

The gift was a box of See's Chocolates. Mixed Nuts and Chews. Dave's favorite.

"Well, open the card," Charlie demanded.

Dave opened the envelope. Two tickets to Tennessee Williams's *The Glass Menagerie* at Arizona Theatre Company slid out. "That's nice," Dave said quietly, his words more polite than heartfelt. Upset, he needed to be alone. "I think I'll change before dinner."

Charlie, oblivious to Dave's mood, trailed after him to the bedroom, talking about the small events of the day. The neighbor he'd met in the supermarket. The noise the kids made after school as they played in the pool, screeching with delight. The dog he'd seen from the small terrace off the kitchen as it walked by with its owner in tow. And then, about the afternoon activities househunting.

"Ronaldo and I checked out a few more houses," Charlie said, as Dave dropped his tie on the bed.

"What'd you think?"

"Honestly, not much."

"Why?" Dave asked, removing his white dress shirt and handing it to Charlie, who in turn, stuffed it into a blue, dry-cleaners bag.

"I didn't really like the neighborhood."

"Then why look there?" Dave wondered. "Just tell Ronaldo the neighborhoods you're interested in." Dave stepped over to the en-suite sink in his briefs and washed his face.

Charlie picked up Dave's slacks, folded them, and slipped them onto a wooden hanger. He hung up the tie on the metal rack inside the closet. He placed the black Cole Haan loafers on the appropriate shelf. "Well, that's the problem," he said, emerging from the closet. "I really don't know the neighborhoods. So, we've been checking out North Central and a lot of houses closer to your office. I know you're concerned about the drive."

"The traffic can be tough," Dave admitted, drying his face with a towel, "but I don't want to live too close to the office. I already spend too much time there."

"Physically and mentally," Charlie added.

"So nothing yet?" Dave stepped into a pair of grey Nike shorts.

"Oh, I've seen nice houses, but they aren't for us."

"Too bad," Dave said, slipping on a dark blue tee shirt sporting the logo of the San Francisco Police Department.

"I thought you were afraid to wear that thing." Charlie had bought the tee shirt at a fundraiser during a Bay Area street fair.

"As long as we're staying in, it's okay. Remember when that woman ran up to me in the city and said she needed my help?" Dave smiled at the memory, suddenly longing to be back in the Bay Area.

"How could I forget?" Charlie let out a chuckle before returning to the subject at hand. "Maybe I'll have better luck tomorrow. We have appointments to see five houses in Scottsdale. We'll see how that goes."

* * *

Delirious from a blood-borne infection, Daisy was admitted to an intensive care unit in the middle of the night. The nurse's aide who coordinated the transfer spotted the note lying on Daisy's bedside table. Glancing at the contents, she handed it to the lead EMT. "Mac, this might come in handy." Mac, a stocky guy sporting a crewcut who had played defensive end in high school, shoved the note in his pocket.

That morning at Denny's, after finishing breakfast, Mac pulled the note out when he reached for his wallet to settle the check. "Crap," he said, reading the note. "I've got to get this back to that old lady." But with his shift over, he had no desire to return to the hospital. Instead, he opted to do the next best thing. He pulled out his cell phone.

"Hello, is this Jack Lee?" Mac asked.

"Speaking."

"I'm afraid I have some bad news for you."

* * *

"Oh my God," Jack said, hanging up the phone. He'd been outside planting miniature cacti when his cell phone rang. "She's in the hospital," he told Enid who was stretched out on a lounge chair sipping lemonade.

"Who?" Enid asked, sitting up with alarm. She wore a white outfit; white top and white shorts; a large straw gardening hat rested in her lap.

"Daisy," Jack answered. He examined her face for any sense of recognition. "The woman we thought might be my aunt."

"Oh," Enid said, seemingly relieved, "is that all." She relaxed back into the lounger. Though she'd told Jack she'd help with the planting, after opening the first bag of fertilizer, the smell had put her off.

"She's ill," Jack said, his voice tinged with annoyance. "Here we have a chance to get to know her, and now it gets complicated."

But Enid still didn't seem to care. "That's too bad Jack," she said, checking her manicure. "Jack, we really should have hired someone to do the gardening. It's such a messy job."

Jack wiped the sweat from his forehead. He hated when Enid changed the subject in mid-discussion. Irritated, he ignored her behavior. "Do you think we should go visit her?"

Enid offered a perplexed look. "I don't see why. We don't know her. This seems to be a private matter. What does she have to do with us?"

Jack arched a brow. "I don't know exactly, but if she's my father's sister, I should do something."

"Oh no." Enid waved her hands in the air. "We're not taking on the care of an old woman, someone we've never even met. Forget it."

"Then again, she might not be my aunt," Jack said, his face registering a modicum of relief. "That certainly is possible."

"That's right," Enid agreed. "She probably isn't."

"It would be too much of a coincidence, don't you think?" Jack caught sight of an eagle soaring in the distance. The graceful majesty of the bird reminded him of his Dad's love for everything Southwest. "No . . . I'm going over to the hospital," he reconsidered. "I better just go."

Enid sneered. "And what do you think that'll prove?"

"I don't know," Jack said. "It just feels like the right thing to do."

Enid pressed her lips together. "Okay, but if you're going . . . I'm going with you. Give me a few minutes to change my clothes. You're too soft-hearted for your own good, Jack Lee. Much too soft-hearted."

* * *

Daisy's eyes felt like hot coals. She'd tossed and turned, confused, uncertain where she was. She'd tried to remove the IV from her wrist when the ICU nurse entered the cubicle to check Daisy's vitals. Daisy struggled, certain the woman wearing a facemask had come to kill her.

But by nine o'clock in the morning, her fever had broken. Exhausted, she napped on and off.

She was awakened by a gentle touch to her arm. A nurse hovered nearby. "Good afternoon, sweetie. Are you awake?" Her voice was like honey. "Do you remember me?"

Daisy smiled, hoping that was enough recognition.

"I need you to tell me your name and birth date, if you can."

"I'm Daisy Lee," she managed to get out. She then provided her birthdate.

"Good, very good." The nurse smiled and patted her shoulder. "I have a few more questions for you. There's a gentleman here who says he might be your nephew. Do you have a nephew?"

"I don't have any children," Daisy answered, shaking her head from side-to-side, eyes closed.

"No, dear," the nurse tried again. "A nephew. A man named Jack Allen Lee?"

Daisy drifted off.

The nurse touched her arm. Daisy opened her eyes. "Can you tell me the name of your brother?" she asked.

"Jacob," Daisy replied weakly. "Jacob. Is he here?" she asked somewhat confused, her eyes searching about.

"His son is," the nurse answered.

"Oh." Daisy nodded off again.

"Ms. Lee," the nurse gently called as she stroked Daisy's hair. "Do you know a Jack Allen Lee?"

Daisy's head cleared for a moment. "Yes," she nodded, eyes wide open.

"Is he your nephew?"

"Jack," she murmured. She smiled broadly.

The nurse adjusted Daisy's head on the pillow. "There you go, dear. Now you rest."

* * *

Jack took a seat in the cramped medical director's office. The desk was a mess. Freebies from pharmaceutical companies, blank pads and pens embossed with names like Merck and Pfizer were mixed in with scattered pink and yellow papers, and a variety of tiny mechanical windup cars and robots. A white coffee mug with red *We Love You Grandpa* lettering, still a quarter full with black coffee, rested on an open copy of the latest edition of the *New England Journal of Medicine*. Jack wondered how anyone could work in such surroundings. Enid had gone to the restroom. He glanced repeatedly out the open door to the hallway, hoping to catch a glimpse of her as she walked by.

Dr. Mueller, a balding man in his late sixties with fine white hair and a large bulbous nose, shifted a stack of medical records from his chair to the floor near his feet so that he might sit down. "Excuse the mess," he apologized. "I'm the chairman of the hospital's quality committee. I have to review these cases before our next meeting on Friday morning."

Jack nodded in sympathy as if he understood. "My wife should be here any moment," he said, shifting the conversation as he continued to look toward the door. "I'd prefer if we waited for her before we begin. I'm not very good with all of this."

Mueller looked at his watch. "Well, I don't have much time. If it's okay with you . . ."

"Over here," Jack called, spotting Enid.

She stopped midstep. While Jack wore an old pair of jeans with a cotton shirt of bold, red and blue stripes, Enid had dressed for the occasion in a sophisticated olive green dress and white sandals, full makeup and gold jewelry.

Enid took a seat.

"We've spoken to your aunt," Mueller started.

Jack's tone revealed his excitement. "So we *are related*?"

"Ms. Lee confirmed her brother's name was indeed Jacob. And she did recognize your name."

"Really," Jack said enthusiastically. "Are there any other family members? Children?"

Mueller shook his head. "We have no next of kin."

"She never married?"

"We don't know her full history. We just know she's currently single." Mueller's face was stoic.

"When might we be able to talk with her?" Jack asked.

"Her condition is very serious. These superbugs are hard to knock out. She's barely holding her own, though I'm happy to say her fever has come down and she's no longer delirious. We should know more in a few days."

"Oh," was all that Jack could manage.

Mueller lifted the coffee mug, tilted it, looked inside, and then returned it to the desk. "You understand that you have no legal rights to make any healthcare decisions on her behalf."

"Of course not," Jack answered, surprised at the turn of the discussion. "We just wanted to know if she was indeed my aunt."

Afterward, as he and Enid waited for the elevator, Jack was deep in thought. Stepping into the elevator, he couldn't help but acknowledge the obvious, "It's really crazy. I never met my father's sister, and now I have the opportunity, but she may not survive. It's the damnedest thing."

Enid, who'd been quiet and pensive, brightened. "You're probably her only living relative, Jack. If she dies, there could be an inheritance."

Jack was aghast. Leave it to Enid to be focused on money.

"Jack, you might inherit her estate. We could trade up to a bigger Biltmore property. A home in Taliverde. Those homes are one-of-a-kind." There was a gleam in Enid's eye. "This could be quite a windfall."

"Taliverde is well beyond our means," Jack countered, annoyed by Enid's suggestion. "The monthly association dues alone are more than we can afford."

"Daisy's house must be worth some money. I wonder how she had the means to settle in the Biltmore. She must have a sizeable nest egg."

"Enid, I don't think we should be counting her money. After all, we're strangers. For all I know she's living on Social Security."

"Jack, that's ridiculous. No one in the Biltmore is living on Social Security."

"You don't think so?"

"Tomorrow, I'm going to find a lawyer who can advise us."

"I'm not comfortable with this," Jack admitted as they walked through the hospital lobby. "I feel like a vulture."

"Someone has to help her," Enid argued. "She's all alone. She may need us to make medical decisions. We might need a power of attorney. We have a lot to do."

"It's all happening too fast," Jack said, as they crossed the parking lot toward their car.

"And tomorrow, we're going to ask Sheila for the key to Daisy's house. I want to see her place."

"She's not going to give us the key," Jack insisted.

"Oh yes she will," Enid assured him. "You just leave that discussion to me. I'll get those keys and we'll see that house. Mark my words."

Jack had no doubt. Enid could be a dog with a bone, especially when money was involved. As Jack backed out of the spot, his cell phone rang. He fumbled for it in his pocket. "Yes," he said, listening carefully to the other party on the line. "Okay, we're coming back."

"Who was that?" Enid asked.

"The hospital. She's gone into convulsions."

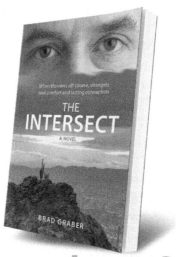

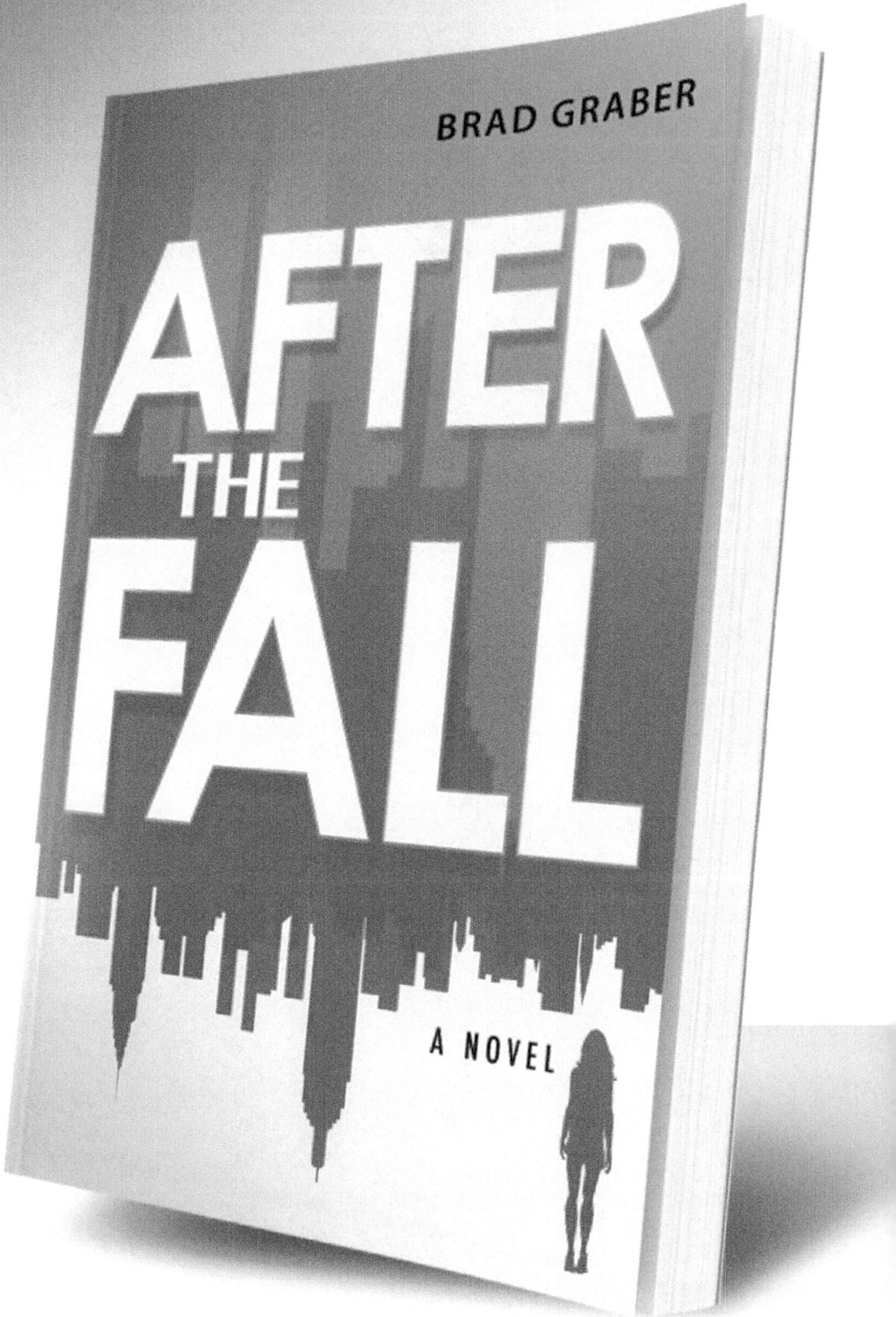
BRAD GRABER
AFTER THE FALL
A NOVEL

THE SECRETS FAMILIES KEEP.
THE LIES THEY TELL.

"... a fast-paced and moving novel about family, memory, and love that will appeal to all readers who appreciate good storytelling and especially well-drawn characters."—**Indie Reader**

"Graber explores the themes of family, identity, and the importance of being connected, with a strong appeal to readers who enjoy sleuth, adventure, and stories with emotional and psychological depth."...**Readers' Favorite**

Winner of a **2019 Indie Reader Discovery Award, Forward Indies Finalist,** and a **Colorado Independent Publishers Association Book Award.**

 FOR THE FIRST 2 CHAPTERS OF

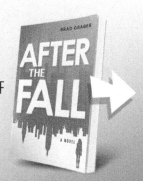

1

Rikki braced herself as the traffic light at 73rd Avenue and Parson's Boulevard turned yellow. With one hand on the dashboard and the other gripping the door handle, she held her breath as her grandmother leaned forward and stepped on the gas. Three pigeons in the road broke into flight as the red Ford Mustang blasted through the intersection.

Rikki was furious. "Why did you do that?" she yelled. "Didn't you see those birds? You could have hurt them."

An overcast November morning in Queens, New York, and Rikki was being driven to school by her grandmother, Rita Goldenbaum. The weekend had been unusually cold, and by late Sunday afternoon, dark clouds had released the season's first snowfall. Now the temperatures were just above freezing, and the powdery white that had earlier beautified the brick and cement neighborhood had turned gray and messy in Monday morning's rush hour.

Rita let out an exuberant laugh. Her bright red hair, set in curlers and wrapped in a clear plastic kerchief, matched the chipped nail polish on her chubby hands. Rikki thought the color particularly unbecoming on a woman of Rita's age. "Honey, don't you know pigeons are just rats with wings? Filthy animals spreading disease wherever they go." A lit cigarette dangled from the corner of Rita's mouth, bobbing with each word.

Rikki rolled her eyes. "Why do you have to be so mean?" she said as she waved a hand to clear the air of cigarette smoke. "When are you going to stop that filthy habit? It's 2005 and you're still smoking."

"Mean?" Rita's voice was pure innocence as she shifted the cigarette from her mouth to her left hand. "There's not a mean bone in my body."

Never mind, Rikki thought, disgusted. She wasn't in the mood to play Rita's game.

"No, seriously," Rita said, slipping the tip of the Salem 100 out a slim opening of the driver's side window. A bit of ash flew off. "I really want to know. What did I say that was so terrible?" She looked over at Rikki. Her large brown eyes feigned concern as the car drifted from its lane.

Rikki had come to accept Rita as a complicated woman with many opinions, the chief of which was that life was unfair. A native New Yorker, born and raised in the Bronx, Rita spoke her mind. Whether her opinions were obnoxious, outrageous, or conventional, she wore them like a badge of honor. There was no filter. If it was on the brain, it came out the mouth.

"You know perfectly well what I'm talking about," Rikki said. She hated Rita's pretense almost as much as she hated her smoking.

Rita's voice rose an octave. "About vermin?"

Rikki shifted. "About everything. You're so negative."

"I'm edgy," Rita insisted, eyes focused on the road. "New Yorkers are sharp and sarcastic. That's just the way it is. I'd have thought by now, after years of living here, you'd be over all that Michigan niceness." She sniffed, as if being polite was to be avoided at all costs. "You're still not one of us. My goodness." Rita took a drag off her cigarette. "You're one stubborn young lady."

"I'll never be a New Yorker," Rikki muttered, a sadness gripping her heart as she rolled down her window to let in some fresh air.

The Mustang stopped at a red light. "Now honey, don't get all emotional on me." Rita's tone softened. "You've got to grow a thicker skin to survive in this world. Trust me. I know. I'm the expert," she boasted. "You know that I love you. Right?"

Rikki took a deep breath. Whenever they had words, Rita defaulted to pronouncements of love.

"Oh no," Rita said with a chortle as the light changed to green. "If you don't think I love you, you must really be mad. What else can I say, my darling? I keep forgetting. I have a very serious granddaughter."

Rikki barely listened as Rita rattled on. Her thoughts shifted to the upcoming day. High school had proved a hard adjustment. A junior, she was still struggling to fit in. There were so many students, and for a shy girl it was simply overwhelming. As the car approached a stop sign, Rikki grew increasingly anxious. Queens Hospital loomed ahead. They were at the halfway point. Soon she'd be in front of the school.

Rita let out a hacking cough, easing up on the gas before clearing her throat and once again accelerating. "And here I am, encouraging all your nonsense," she said, cigarette held high in the air as she took a deep breath. "You should be taking the bus like the other kids. You know your problem?" Rita lectured. "You've been raised like a fragile doll. Well, you're just like everyone else. The sooner you realize it, the better we'll all be. That imagination of yours …"

"I didn't imagine it," Rikki quickly defended herself. "It happened."

Rita waved the cigarette as if, by doing so, she could dismiss Rikki's truth. "Whatever happened, you've made too much of it … just like you always do. A big brouhaha over nothing."

Rikki pressed her eyes tightly shut. *Why did Rita have to bring it up again?* At the end of her sophomore year, walking to catch the bus in the morning, she'd been accosted by a young man. At first she thought he was going to ask for directions. He blocked her path forward. When he grabbed her by the arm, she became hysterical, dropping her schoolbooks and struggling with him until he let her go. She ran all the way home.

The encounter had only intensified her fear of strangers.

"This is such a safe neighborhood," Rita insisted as they passed a group of teenagers huddled at the corner, waiting for the light to change. "Look at them," she pointed. Two of the four were in the midst of a pushing match. The smaller one tripped and dropped to a knee, struggling to break his fall. "They're laughing and horsing around. Doing all the things kids do. Do they look afraid?"

Clearly, they were picking on the little kid. Rikki peered to see if she recognized any of the faces. No. None of them looked familiar.

"You should be over this nonsense by now," Rita griped. "I shouldn't have to drive you to school every day."

"I can't help it," Rikki answered, mindful that she was still uncomfortable negotiating the streets of Queens.

Rita repeated her familiar mantra. "There are lots of people in this world. The quicker you learn that, the better."

But Rikki couldn't help but be afraid. The borough of Queens was a giant melting pot of skin colors, religions, and ethnicities. Blacks, Hispanics, and whites. Jews, Italians, Indians, Greeks, and Vietnamese. More diversity than Rikki had ever been exposed to in suburban Detroit, where most everyone had been white.

"I know," Rikki meekly answered as they stopped for another light. Two boys ran past them, a third in close pursuit.

"You should be riding the bus," Rita repeated as they passed a bus stop where a group of children waited.

Rikki hated taking public transportation. The bus during the morning rush hour was too densely packed. If she was unable to get a seat, she dreaded touching the germ-covered metal poles, and she held her breath as strangers pushed past her, not wanting to breathe in their exhalations. As the bus bounced up and down, bags, umbrellas, and, sometimes, wandering hands rubbed up against her.

"There's no reason to be afraid," Rita insisted. The red tip of her cigarette glowed brightly as she took another drag.

But Rikki *was* afraid. Since moving in with her grandmother, she'd struggled to adjust to the world around her. Now and then, she'd have a glimpse of a happier time. But it was merely the dimmest of memories. The doctors had promised it would all come back eventually, but so far it hadn't. She had a terrible sense of a *before* and *after*, in which Queens was most definitely the *after*. And yet she did have flashes of recall about a life in Michigan. A lovely two-story brick house on a quiet, tree-lined street. A flagstone walkway that led up to a front door the color of gingerbread. Such memories contrasted sharply with the high-rise buildings that now surrounded her. The cement sidewalks that choked any bit of greenery from the landscape. When she asked Rita about what was wrong with her, Rita would become annoyed.

"Rikki, we've been through this, over and over. There's nothing wrong with you. You just need to live in the present. That's all we've got. This moment. No more."

"I want to go back to the doctor," Rikki had begged.

"That psychiatrist was a quack," Rita had insisted. "You're done with all that now. I won't have you up at night crying because you think something's wrong. You've just had an *emotional upset*. Plenty of people lose their mothers when they're young. Madonna. Rosie O'Donnell. They've gone on to have successful lives. And so will you."

Given time, the crying did eventually stop. As puberty kicked in, Rikki's body changed, and so did her focus. Looking in the mirror, she cringed at her oily skin, untamed wavy brown hair, and hopelessly oval face. The small gap between her two front teeth made her unwilling to smile. Convinced that she wasn't pretty, she'd recently gained weight, and because her breasts were still not fully developed, her figure remained awkward. She hid herself in oversized, baggy clothing. The bigger, the better. *I look like Darlene Conner from "Roseanne,"* she thought. *A cross between a tomboy and a mess.*

"I told your mother that living in that lily-white suburb was a bad idea," Rita said as the car hit a pothole and bounced. "But your mother was so set in her ways. *'Detroit isn't lily white,'* she'd say. 'Maybe not,' I'd tell her. 'But Birmingham, Michigan, sure is.'"

"It wasn't *all* white," Rikki protested, eager to defend the mother she couldn't quite remember.

"It may be green in the summer," Rita snapped, "but Birmingham, Michigan, is white, white, and white. It might be a lovely place to live, I'll give you that, but it's not the real world. The real world is Queens."

"No," Rikki whispered as she rebelled at Rita's assertion. "That's *your* world."

"Don't be fresh," Rita snapped as the light ahead turned yellow. "I still have my hearing, thank you very much."

Rikki braced herself. "You better slow down."

Rita gunned it, just barely making it through as the light turned red.

"Stop telling me how to drive!" Rita complained. "My goodness. How about we listen to the radio? Maybe that'll get *your mind off of the road.*" She reached over and fumbled with the dials, ash dropping onto the leather console.

Rikki pushed her grandmother's hand away as the car drifted from its lane. "I'll do it. Pay attention to your driving."

With the turn of a knob, Rush Limbaugh's voice bathed the car in warm, somber tones as he discussed the recent election of Angela Merkel as the first female Chancellor of Germany. Rikki winced. "How can you listen to him? He gives me the creeps."

Rita took another drag on her cigarette. It was getting down to the end. "You know I love Rush. Next to Bill O'Reilly, he's the only one who can make any sense of this crazy world."

"But he's a drug addict," Rikki insisted. "All that doctor-shopping for prescriptions."

"That poor man was in pain. You don't know what it's like. When you're older, everything hurts. And when a doctor prescribes painkillers, you're supposed to take them."

"I thought you weren't old." Rikki smirked as she turned off the radio in the middle of Rush's diatribe about a new Iraqi constitution. "Maybe I should call you *Grandma* from now on?"

"Don't you dare," Rita flared, taking her eyes off the road just long enough to offer her granddaughter a sharp glare and pass her what remained of her Salem 100. "Now stop teasing me and get rid of this."

Rikki took the smoking stub from her grandmother's outstretched fingers. She rolled the passenger window down. "You promised you'd stop smoking."

"I know," Rita said.

"How about making that your 2006 New Year's resolution?"

Rita shrugged a shoulder.

"It's such a disgusting habit," Rikki said as she tossed the butt out the passenger window at the precise moment that a gust of wind spiraled the hot poker back into the car. "Oh, my God," Rikki screamed, wildly flailing, lifting herself up, arching her back, struggling against the seatbelt that was secured about her waist.

"What?" Rita yelled, as she looked over at Rikki. "Are you okay?"

The car bounced up onto the curb. Rita let out an "Oh, my God," as she struggled to straighten the wheel. Back on the road again, she overcorrected, sending the Mustang into a spin. As Rita and Rikki screamed, the car spun across two lanes, crossing the median, before coming to rest parallel to oncoming traffic.

◆

Harry Aldon was tired. He hated getting up early to walk the dog. But, living in Phoenix, Arizona, that's what he needed to do. Tender paws burnt easily on superheated pavement, and even though it was mid-November, and the intense triple-digit summer heat had long since dissipated, dogs are creatures of habit with built-in alarm clocks and a demand for consistent routine. At six a.m. Harry opened his eyes. Beetle, his wire-haired fox terrier, was wide awake and whining. The little dog's torso was pressed up against the adjacent pillow. His head rested on his two front paws as he stared into Harry's eyes.

Harry blinked.

Beetle stretched, thrusting his little body back into a downward-dog position before standing up on the bed with a brisk shake.

"Okay, okay," Harry groaned. "I'm getting up."

Harry lifted Beetle off the bed. "Good boy," Harry said as sixteen pounds of squirming energy wiggled intently in his arms. He lowered Beetle to the carpet. "No more jumping for you, old friend. We've got to keep you intact."

Grabbing a pair of black Nike gym shorts and an old gray T-shirt, Harry lumbered into the bathroom to wash his face. A nearby night-light offered the softest of illumination as he looked into the mirror. He was nearly fifty-five years old. Still vigorous. Still lean. His blue eyes clear and bright. Tiny wrinkles were just beginning to appear about his eyes and his mouth, and despite his age, he remained surprised by their presence. His dark gray curly hair, a crushed bed mess, had recently turned an interesting salt and pepper, making him, he believed, appear even older. He ran a hand through the thick curls, pushing them away from his face, only to watch as they bounced back and covered his forehead.

"Got you, buddy," he said, lifting Beetle up and carrying him off to the garage where he attached a leash to the terrier's collar. Beetle's tongue hung out of his mouth as he panted with excitement. Harry could feel the dog's rapid heartbeat in the palm of his hand.

With Beetle's collar secured, Harry pushed the button to raise the garage door. It was dark outside. The cool November air embraced Harry and Beetle as they made their way through the Arizona Biltmore neighborhood. The sweet scent of new winter grass, freshly planted and watered by early-morning automatic sprinklers, flooded Harry's senses as he strolled quickly behind Beetle, who, despite his advanced years, seemed fiercely energized by the morning hour.

As he turned a corner on the path, a distant figure loomed. Harry closed his eyes. He wished he didn't have to run into anyone at such an early hour. It was hard to be congenial when the power of conversation seemed beyond him.

"Hello!" called the figure of a woman, waving, as dawn began to break in the east.

"Hello," Harry politely said, alarmed that his tongue seemed stuck to the roof of his mouth.

It was Lil. Lil Turner. He'd run into her off and on for the last few weeks. Lil was new to the neighborhood. She'd introduced herself one morning as Harry rambled by, quite oblivious to her perky figure. Though she tended to wear her shoulder-length blonde hair tucked behind her ears, on this particular morning it was rolled tightly in a bun high atop her head. With no makeup, and in her fitted, pink yoga outfit, flat midriff fully exposed, Lil appeared much younger than her fifty years.

"It should be a beautiful day," Lil offered, examining the sky. She held a newspaper, wrapped up tightly in plastic, like a baton.

Harry nodded, hoping he might pass Lil without much interaction.

"You're awfully quiet this morning," Lil said, as Beetle sniffed her fluffy pink slippers. "Hey there, Beetle, you sweet thing. How are *you* this morning?"

Harry wondered what Beetle might do if he ever got hold of those slippers.

"I just woke up," Harry said in his own defense. "I'm not much for talk in the morning."

Lil laughed. "Oh, Harry Aldon. You're such a dud."

"Thank you, Lil," Harry said as he pushed past. "So nice of you to say."

Lil laughed again. "Honestly, *some men*," she called out.

Harry looked back and waved, hoping to signal the end of the interaction.

"Do you have plans for lunch?" Lil called, hands on her hips, newspaper tucked under her arm.

"I'm working on my novel," Harry said.

Unable to take a hint, she continued. "So, you're not going to eat?"

Harry shook his head no.

"What's a girl to do?" she asked, disappointment heavy in her voice.

Harry ignored her as Beetle humped his back, taking care of business. Harry bent down with a plastic bag as Beetle took two steps forward and kicked some loose dirt backward, catching Harry in the face. "Jesus," Harry yelled, yanking on the leash. But Beetle offered one more kick before wandering over to sniff a nearby bush.

"That's rich," Lil laughed as she strolled over to Harry. "Someday that dog is going to kick something worse than dirt in your face, Harry Aldon. And you'll deserve it." She wagged her newspaper, like an index finger, at him. "Women don't like men who play games."

Harry blushed. "I don't know what you're talking about, Lil."

"Oh, yes, you do," she insisted, turning sideways in a provocative pose.

Harry sighed. "Lil…it is six a.m. Give me a break."

And then, as if on cue, Beetle whined. He was ready to continue the walk. It was time to move on.

◆

"Are you okay?" Rita asked, clutching the steering wheel of the car.

A large city bus had stopped just short of the passenger side. The bus driver glared down at them through the bus windshield. Rikki looked away, embarrassed by the man's angry face.

"Yes," Rikki answered, her mouth dry, her nerves shaken. She reached between her legs and retrieved the cigarette butt, now extinguished, and pitched it out the window. "I have a hole in my jeans," she said, poking about with her finger. "I think I burned my leg."

Car horns blew as Rita revved into action. She shifted into reverse and slowly backed up, maneuvering the car until it was in the correct lane and facing the right direction. More horns blared as she shifted into drive. "Keep your goddamn shirts on," Rita shrieked, as if any of the other drivers could hear her. She accelerated, reaching twenty-five miles per hour before pulling her foot back off the pedal.

"You should pull over and let everyone pass," Rikki suggested, turning around to see the line of cars behind them.

"If I do, you'll never get to school," Rita said, even though she did as Rikki suggested. As the cars whizzed by, Rita held up a middle finger to the driver side window and wildly shouted, "Here's a present for you!"

Rikki blushed crimson. "If it hadn't been for that cigarette…" She decided there wasn't any point in saying any more. Her heart pounded as she relived the car's spinning. She'd never liked amusement park rides. They made her nauseous.

"I know," Rita quickly agreed.

"Then why?" Rikki blurted out, unable to contain herself. "Everyone knows cigarettes cause cancer. How can you still be smoking?"

She'd asked the same question the night before when she caught Rita sitting on the terrace, a cigarette burning brightly.

Rita opened her mouth as if she were about to speak, but nothing came out. Arching her eyebrows, she seemed to struggle to find the right words. "It's such a hard habit to break. I've been doing it for so many years."

Rikki thought she made no sense. "So, when are you going to stop?"

"I can stop anytime I want," Rita quickly answered, a lilt to her voice as the car once again entered the flow of traffic. "Stopping isn't the issue … I've stopped a thousand times. It's *quitting* that's tough."

Typical Rita, Rikki thought, irritated. *Not taking any of this seriously.*

"Trust me," Rita went on. "If I could, I would. It's so darn expensive. When I think of the money I've wasted on those cigarettes…" Rita shook her head. "It just makes my blood boil. But I'm addicted. Maybe we should look on the bright side. It could have been heroin."

Rikki was shocked. "You've tried heroin?"

"I didn't say *I tried it,*" Rita said indignantly. "But if I had, I'm sure it would have been worse than these damn cigarettes."

Rikki couldn't help laughing. It was the kind of absurd remark Rita was especially adept at. And despite all of Rita's failings and Rikki's struggles with her, there were moments of levity that they shared. Rita could be entertaining. That, and the fact that Rikki had nowhere else to go. Rita was *home.*

"I hope you won't be too mad at your old grandma," Rita offered, her tone sincere and contrite even as she referred to herself in a way that Rikki couldn't.

"You only say 'grandma' when you're trying to manipulate me," Rikki pointed out.

Rita smiled. "See. You're just like me. Sharp as a tack. No one can pull the wool over your eyes."

Rikki doubted that was true. Her grandmother was just humoring her.

"I'm proud of you," Rita said, turning to give Rikki a warm smile. "You're an intelligent girl. You mark my words. Being smart will come in handy. Let the other girls be pretty and silly. Not my Rikki. You keep to your studies, and someday, you'll be a big success."

If Rita had taken a knife and stabbed Rikki, it couldn't have been more painful. Rikki was convinced that Rita thought she wasn't pretty.

"Now let's get you to school," Rita said as Queens High came into view.

◆

"Let me off over there." Rikki pointed to the corner.

"Don't be silly," Rita answered. "I'll drop you in front of the school."

"No, here," Rikki insisted. "I'll walk the rest of the way."

Rita shrugged. "Anyone would think you were embarrassed to be seen with me." She patted the plastic kerchief encasing her spoolies. "Is it my hair? Is that the problem?" She peered into the rear-view mirror.

Rikki sighed. Some truths were best conveyed with silence.

"Okay, no one has to tell me the score. Wait till you're my age," Rita said as she pulled over to the curb. "You think it's easy being Miss Queens, the reigning beauty of the neighborhood?" She barely controlled a guffaw. "You have to work hard to look this good."

"I'm sure," Rikki said as she dismissed her grandmother, who was now boldly laughing. She leaned over and gave Rita a fast peck on the cheek. "I'll see you later. Thanks for the ride." She stepped out of the car and slammed the door behind her. Looking back, she could see Rita inside, wildly waving.

As she walked through the gates and up the stairs of Queens High, Rikki merged into the rush of students. The hallways were packed. Slightly out of breath from climbing to the third floor, Rikki headed to first-period English. She was relieved to finally slip into the classroom. Among the crush of students, she'd felt intensely uncomfortable. Was she moving too slowly? Too fast? Not pretty enough? Was she taking up too much space in the hallway? Gnawing self-doubts were always with her, but nowhere as magnified, or as powerful, as in the halls of Queens High.

The class had been reading Dreiser's *An American Tragedy,* and Rikki had a well-worn used copy atop her books. Rita had taken it out of the library. "There's no point in buying a new book," Rita had scolded, "when there's a perfectly good library nearby."

Rikki had read well ahead, eager to be absorbed into the burgeoning love affair. But the book was nothing like the movie *A Place in the Sun,* with Elizabeth Taylor and Montgomery Clift, which she'd watched breathlessly with Rita on Turner Classic Movies. In the film, the characters' names were different, and Rikki didn't recognize much from the novel. *Would they ever get to the love story?* she wondered, her fingers dancing on the cover of the thick paperback.

Mr. Rosenfeld, a middle-aged man with gray hair and a matching mustache and goatee, stood at the front of the class and waited for the last of the stragglers to take their seats. He was dressed in a bright red sweater, a light blue shirt, and a black bow tie with white polka dots. The sternness of his manner contrasted wildly with the boldness of his clothing choices as he assessed the students before him.

As soon as the bell sounded, Mr. Rosenfeld began expounding on Dreiser's narrative, and though Rikki was enjoying the novel, a certain sleepiness came over her. When Mr. Rosenfeld turned his back to the class and began to write on the blackboard, Rikki was thinking about handsome Montgomery Clift. She jumped when her daydream was interrupted by a tap on the shoulder.

"Rikki, I'll meet you in the cafeteria for lunch later," Barbra whispered from behind. "I have something important to ask."

Rikki turned around.

Barbra Winer smiled, revealing a mouth full of silver. Her hair, dyed a gothic black, was piled high atop her head, knotted loosely, strands falling here and there. She wore dark red lipstick, which clashed with her olive-green blouse covered in ruffles.

Rikki thought she looked like a pirate in a beehive hairdo.

"That girl's on her way to becoming a tramp," Rita had said on more than one occasion when Barbra had visited. "That rat's nest. And those clothes. And the way she swoons over boys. Her mother needs to get that one in hand," Rita had warned Rikki, a finger in the air. "You mark my words. She's bad news."

Rikki had given up reminding Rita that Barbra's mother was long dead.

Barbra leaned forward, arms resting on the desk, stretching herself forward awkwardly. "It's a gift from my stepmother," she said defensively as Rikki's eyes fell upon one of her sleeves. "She *forced* me to wear it today." Barbra made a face as if a bad odor had come over her. "Isn't it perfectly awful? I tried to say no, but *she kept pushing*. And you know how she is. If I don't do what she wants, she talks with my father. It was just easier to wear it." Barbra shrugged as if it was all fine.

Rikki nodded that she understood, but if Rita had ever made her wear such an ugly blouse, she was certain she'd skip school altogether and spend the rest of the day in Flushing Meadows Park roaming the empty pavilions that had once hosted the 1964 New York World's Fair. Rikki loved the park with its iron spheres and weathered pavilions. So peaceful and quiet.

Mr. Rosenfeld was done at the board and called the class back to order by tapping a wooden pointer on the edge of his desk. Rikki joined the others as she spun about to full attention.

"Can anyone," Mr. Rosenfeld asked, his voice edged with excitement as he looked out at the assembled class of juniors, "tell me what Dreiser's motivation might have been for telling this particular story?" He held the hardcopy of Dreiser's book pressed to his chest.

There was silence.

"Well, it certainly is a wonderful story," he said with a big grin. "It's a classic tale of America. The hopes and dreams of a young man who struggles to better himself. So today," and Mr. Rosenfeld turned to the chalkboard where he'd written out the word *IDENTITY* in capital letters, "we're going to discuss identity—who we are as Americans, and what it means to be an American in Dreiser's world."

Rikki felt herself growing impatient. She didn't want to talk about

Dreiser's America. What was the point? How could a discussion about another time and place be instructive? She started to doodle mindlessly in her open notebook.

"So let's begin," Mr. Rosenfeld said, his voice rising to an excited pitch. "Who'd like to start? Who can tell me what is driving Clyde to leave Kansas City?"

The classroom was quiet. Rikki drew a dinosaur that looked an awful lot like Dino from *The Flintstones*. Then she heard her name being called. Startled, she looked up to find Mr. Rosenfeld standing before her, looking down.

"Rikki, let's start with you. What do you think? Why does Clyde want to leave Kansas City?"

"Well," she began, "he's unhappy."

"Yes," Mr. Rosenfeld nodded. "But a lot of people are unhappy. That doesn't necessarily make them leave home."

"But there's nothing for him there," she said somewhat indignantly, her heart beating rapidly, hoping that Mr. Rosenfeld might turn his attention elsewhere. "It all seemed so hopeless."

"Is that the only reason?" Mr. Rosenfeld asked, his blue eyes looking through her.

Rikki thought for a moment. "And he was running away from that accident. The car hit a little girl and killed her. And even though he wasn't driving, Clyde was afraid he might be prosecuted."

Mr. Rosenfeld nodded his approval.

"But he was *always* afraid…" Rikki continued, as she realized the motivation of the character. "Afraid he'd never rise above his parents' station in life. That he'd always be the poor son of missionaries. Trapped in a life that he didn't want."

"Yes," Mr. Rosenfeld smiled, shifting his attention from Rikki to the class. "Dreiser is exploring the class system in America. And this is but one story of a young man who wants more." He raised the book high in the air. "Clyde represents everyman. He's all of us," Mr. Rosenfeld declared, just as his wrist suddenly gave way and the thick novel plummeted to the floor, landing hard on his foot.

Nervous giggles filled the classroom.

"Okay, everyone," he said as he attempted to restore order, an expression of intense pain on his face. "Start reading the assignment for tonight, and I'll be right back." And with an awkward step and hop, and then two larger hops, he left the classroom.

◆

"How's he doing?" Harry asked Dr. Newbar.

Harry held Beetle in place as the little dog squirmed on the vet's steel examining table, head hidden under Harry's arm, butt toward Newbar. Harry stroked Beetle's hindquarters in a steady motion, trying to calm him.

"Good," Newbar announced, removing the stethoscope from Beetle's underbelly and looking up. His kind hazel eyes belied his formal demeanor. The certificates on the wall indicated that he'd graduated from veterinary school with high honors and yet he was as easy to talk with as any average Joe on the street. "Everything seems normal," he said, patting Beetle on his haunch. "Of course, he still has that heart murmur."

"He's had that since he was a puppy," Harry pointed out.

Newbar nodded. "As for the coughing, I think it's just a little choking. Dogs get it as they age. It happens to people, too. We begin to forget to fully swallow. Hasn't that ever happened to you?" Newbar asked, then, without waiting for Harry to answer, added "So we cough."

Harry took in the news. "So I'm worried about nothing?"

Newbar broke into a big grin. "At least for today. Yes."

"Oh, good," Harry said, then lifted Beetle off the table and nestled him in his arms. "See, boy, it's nothing to worry about."

Harry breathed a sigh of relief. Working at home, he'd come to rely on Beetle to keep him on schedule. The life of a writer can be all-consuming; once the imagination is fired, the world melts away. But Beetle kept Harry grounded, connected. One yelp and Harry knew it was time to take Beetle out. A whine and Harry grabbed a treat stored in a blue jar embossed with the word "Cookies" that sat on his credenza.

If it weren't for Beetle … and Richard … Harry was certain he'd be completely isolated from the rest of the world. *Good news,* he thought, as he stood at his vet's checkout counter waiting for his credit card to clear. *Richard, we're so lucky. It was nothing at all. Just a cough.*

◆

Rikki hurried along the school corridor, pushed forward by the crowd. Everyone seemed to be speaking at once. A cacophony echoed through the building, making it impossible even to recognize the English language in the babble. It was noon and Rikki's next period was lunch. She stopped at her hall locker to drop off her books. Pressed up against the cold metal, she twisted out her locker combination, glancing over at the nearby trophy case. She was grateful for the glass display. Without its presence, she doubted she'd be able to find her locker so quickly.

"Rikki, can I have a word with you before you go to lunch?"

Mr. Rosenfeld had followed her.

She glanced at her watch. "Sure," she said as she placed her books in the locker, holding onto the brown lunch bag. She turned to give him her full attention.

"I've been impressed with your work in my class. Not only do you have real insight into the literature we're reading, but you're an excellent writer," he said, his smile warm and engaging, "and I think you should consider entering the District's writing contest. It's a $1,000 prize. And it comes with a college scholarship." He winked, his blue eyes sparkling. "You should give it a shot."

Rikki was surprised. She hadn't considered entering. She hadn't thought she really had any talent. And certainly not as a writer. Rita had always stressed the importance of being able to support oneself. Rikki knew that, whatever she did in the future, it had to pay well. *You can't rely on a man,* Rita's voice echoed in her head. *Men come and go.*

Don't wind up like me, working retail… spending your days in lady's shoes. Get an education and become a professional.

Rikki wondered if being a writer paid well.

"You're talented," Mr. Rosenfeld said. "Don't waste it." He hurried off down the hall at the sound of the bell.

Rikki glanced at the trophy case. She wondered about the students whose faces were immortalized behind the glass. Where were they now? Had they achieved their dreams? How had they managed to survive all this confusion? She peered into her open locker. The cold, dark space seemed suddenly warm and inviting. If only she could climb inside, close the door, and hide.

The moment passed.

She headed to the cafeteria with the books she needed for her afternoon classes, a brown paper bag perched precariously on top, pressed to her chest. Navigating her way down the steps to the basement, she kept her eyes cast downward, only looking up when she heard the clanging of metal utensils against casserole-sized serving dishes of lasagna and meat loaf. She gagged at the funky smell: warmed-over spices—cumin, pepper, paprika—mixed with what she thought was a hint of wet dog. Students shuffled in winding lines, trays sliding along. The air squeaked with the high-pitched sound of chairs, metal tips scraping against the linoleum floor.

On the other wall of the cafeteria, she spotted a stack of trays on a conveyor belt. There were remnants of lunches half-eaten—browning apple cores, juice boxes and milk cartons, plastic wrappers entangled with empty chip bags. She swallowed hard, numbing herself to her surroundings as she walked past the cafeteria and into the noisy lunchroom. Mouths moved, bodies twisted and turned; the room was a snake pit of pulsing energy. She was desperate for an open spot in which to settle.

"Rikki," Barbra's voice called, "I'm over here."

Barbra waved Rikki over to a table at the back of the room.

Rikki experienced a terrific sense of relief. She no longer was lost in the crowd. She had escaped the middle of the room, found a place on the periphery.

"I don't see why your grandmother can't also drive *me* to school," Barbra complained. "I promise to be on time."

Rikki picked at a BLT on white toast as Barbra ate out of a plastic container. Some sort of salad which emanated a strong smell of Italian dressing. "You kept her waiting," Rikki reminded her. "She doesn't like to wait."

Barbra wiped her mouth with a napkin. "That happened once. And it was weeks ago."

Rikki shrugged. There wasn't much point in discussing it any further. Once Rita made up her mind, there was nothing she could do.

"You should see me in the morning," Barbra said as she speared a large piece of lettuce and shoved it into her mouth. She continued to talk. "I run all the way to the bus. I keep looking over my shoulder for that man. Tell me again?" she said with a great flurry of drama. "What did he look like?"

Rikki put her sandwich down. She didn't want to think about the assault.

"You should have waited for me that day and there wouldn't have been a problem," Barbra said emphatically. "I'd have kicked him right in the balls."

"Well, good," Rikki said, annoyed that Barbra seemed to view her nightmare as a form of lunchtime entertainment. "Then you should be totally safe walking by yourself in the morning."

"God, Rikki." Barbra rolled her eyes. "What's the point of being best friends if we can't ever talk? You always get mad at me when we talk about this."

Rikki shrugged as she bit into her sandwich. A stringy piece of bacon slid out and dangled from her lips. She quickly pushed the bacon into her mouth, hoping no one other than Barbra had seen her.

Barbra leaned forward, her voice lighter. "So how was homeroom? Did you see him? What was he wearing?"

Rikki pretended innocence, even though she knew darn well what he had worn. A pair of denims and a tight pink shirt, slightly open at the collar. She and Barbra were fixated on the same boy. But she didn't want to appear quite as silly. For Barbra, he wasn't any boy. He was *the boy*. Barney. The boy who made most of the girls in school ignite with excitement.

Rikki had giggled when she first learned his name. "Really? *Barney?* Is he purple? Can he sing and dance? Does he have dinosaur friends?"

Barbra hadn't laughed.

Rikki wiped her mouth. "Yes, I saw him. Tall, dark, and handsome as ever. Nothing's changed since you saw him yesterday."

Rikki and Barbra had been friends for three years... ever since Barbra had moved from Sheepshead Bay in Brooklyn to Queens. A friendship formed less by choice and more by proximity.

"You should get to know her," Rita had suggested. "She just lives three floors below us. You're practically new here. *She's* new here. It seems that you two girls are destined to be friends!"

But Rikki hadn't wanted to befriend Barbra. Not because Rita had made the suggestion, though that alone could be grounds for resisting, but because Barbra seemed too weird. And, being keenly uncomfortable with her own lowly social status among the kids who lived in the building, Rikki had no interest in being friends with a new girl who looked even odder than she did. For Barbra had frizzy, bright orange hair, before she discovered black dye and an iron, and her clothes were desperately in need of replacement, patched here and there. Her elbows and knees appeared darker than the rest of her skin, and there were some days when Rikki picked up an unsavory scent emanating from the new neighbor. In short, Barbra was the perfect dork. A walking, talking carrot stick, in need of a good bath. But Rita was not to be put off, and in her typical boisterous way, she bullied her granddaughter into befriending Barbra. It wasn't until later that Rita changed her mind. But by then it was too late.

Barbra stopped eating, again wiping the corner of her mouth with a napkin. She focused her attention on Rikki as her voice began to rise. "Did Barney talk to you? Say hello?"

Barney Appleton rarely talked … a fact Rikki knew only too well, since she sat next to him in homeroom. She'd made a study of his poor communication skills, often wincing at the way he handled himself. He seemed to struggle with a devastating shyness, surprising in someone so good-looking. He frequently glanced down, offering one-word answers when one word was the least he could say. His favorite utterance seemed to be *yes*, delivered so softly that Rikki was certain she'd mistaken his merely taking a breath for saying the actual word.

Barney hardly spoke to anyone.

He sat quietly, brown wavy hair falling angelically about his ears, framing the angular face with its strong jaw line and high cheekbones. His blue eyes seemed to peek out into the world, oblivious to the powerful effect of his physical presence.

When Barney focused his attention on Rikki, which was rare, she became instantly uncomfortable, desperately wanting his admiration while praying he'd look away and not see the blemish on her nose, or her mismatched sweater and blouse, or an uncontrolled eye twitch, or the one-hundred-and-one flaws she imagined herself to possess every morning when she awoke. *Ugh. I should be in a freak show,* she'd think, all the while desperate to attract Barney's attention.

And though it was hard work to get Barney to talk, it was even harder to sit next to such a handsome boy and say nothing. So Rikki engaged in small talk. She asked questions. Endless questions. And though it was awkward, Rikki soldiered on.

"Isn't it a nice day?" she'd say.

He'd look over and smile.

"Did you walk to school this morning?"

He'd nod affirmatively.

"Would you like a mint?" She blushed. She didn't have any mints. She breathed a sigh of relief when he declined.

It was hopeless. Dull questions followed by uninterested head nods peppered with a *yes* every now and then, before Barney Appleton finally appeared ready to say something. Rikki's heart swooned as

Barney smiled, the corners of his mouth lifting upward to reveal the most beautiful pair of dimples as he formed his precious words. Rikki's world seemed brighter. Time stopped as she glanced at those perfect lips, watched as they parted. She held her breath.

"Aren't *you* nosey," he said, head slightly titled, before turning to look away.

Rikki winced at the memory. "We didn't talk this morning," she lied to Barbra.

"Oh, Rikki…if he was sitting next to me—" She twirled her long black hair about her finger. "—I'd be unable to control myself. He's so freaking gorgeous. I'd probably sit in his lap."

Rikki wondered what that might be like. "No. I don't think I could ever do that," she said, somewhat disappointed in herself.

Barbra sighed, and then offered up a half-eaten powdered donut as the bell rang. It took a moment for Rikki to grab it out of Barbra's fingers. The dusty sugar coating stuck to the roof of her mouth as she gathered up the remnants of her lunch and her book pack and headed off to her next class.

◆

In Phoenix, Lil finished a second cup of green tea, seated at her kitchen counter. The warmth of the liquid calmed her as she closed the newspaper and stared out onto the patio and her small garden filled with potted plants and hanging baskets, where a gray dove perched atop a brown wicker chair. In the summer, Lil enjoyed her tea outdoors before the heat of the sun achieved its full effect. Only recently had she opted for the warmth of the house, as the mornings had grown decidedly cooler with the onset of November.

She checked her cell phone. No new messages. That was good. Her first yoga class was scheduled for eleven o'clock. She still had a few hours.

She wondered if her business partner had arrived on time to open up the studio. The summer morning when Julia had overslept, the place was blazing hot. Lil couldn't help but laugh at the memory of her middle-aged patrons, stretched out in the downward-dog pose, sweating profusely. She had to admit, it seemed like the appropriate punishment for those adults who had let their bodies go to hell. But then, that was back in August when triple-digit temperatures plagued Phoenix.

Yoga had become her second career after working as a grade school teacher in the Phoenix inner city. Eight years of standing in front of a room of seven- and eight-year-olds had proven to be more than she could handle. There had been too many moments when she felt more like a referee than an educator. She hadn't realized until her final year of teaching that she didn't particularly like children. It hit her hard one day when she was struggling to maintain order. Sweet cherubic faces, arms outstretched, vibrating little bodies with mouths constantly moving, desperate to release their pent-up energy. There was no impulse control in the room, and instead of being the person in charge, she'd grown weary of the struggle. Tired of the little hands, the little eyes, and the constant talking, she realized if she didn't do something different, she'd go completely mad.

And so she'd found yoga. And then Julia. And then the yoga studio. And that had been fifteen years ago.

She wiped down the counter as the doorbell chimed. "Who could that be?" she said aloud, tossing the sponge in the sink. She opened her front door in time to see the UPS driver pull away.

Why, she thought, *couldn't it be Ed McMahon with Publisher's Clearinghouse?* If it were, she'd be on her way to the vineyards of Italy or France. Soaking up the beauty of the countryside. Enjoying everything the world of travel had to offer: wine, food, and adventure. And men. Handsome, dark, swarthy men.

She shouted out a "Thank you!" even as the UPS truck disappeared around a turn.

She picked up the small package and pressed it close to her chest as she thought, *At least there are still available men in Phoenix. Like that delicious Harry Aldon.*

The mere thought of her sexy neighbor put a smile on her face.

◆

"We're back," Harry called out as Beetle lumbered over to his water bowl. The house was still. Harry opened the fridge and peeked inside. "Geez," he said, eyes scanning the empty shelves. "I've got to get to the supermarket. There's nothing here."

Check the bin. There's fruit.

It was Richard's voice. Deep, warm, and reassuring. The voice in Harry's head. A voice that he'd used to comfort himself through all the years of loss.

"Oh yeah," Harry answered. He'd put on a few pounds as of late. *A healthy choice... until I get back to the gym.*

The voice. *If you don't take it off now, it'll be harder later.*

Harry had no doubt.

"Beetle's okay," Harry said as he pulled out a Gala apple from the refrigerator and inspected it. Beetle searched the kitchen floor for fallen scraps.

That's good news. It's not his time. But when it is, I'll be there.

Harry was suddenly frightened. *I don't want to think about that,* he thought emphatically, his eyes glistening as he glanced out the kitchen window and spotted a dove waddling along the flagstone around his pool. "Gosh, I love this time of year," he said, changing the subject.

Beetle looked up and cocked his head as if Harry were talking to him.

Harry washed the apple. He reached for a napkin in a large blue bowl decorated with lemons that he and Richard had purchased on a trip to Italy in 1987. Harry fingered the bowl. *We bought this in Portofino? It was a beautiful day. Afterward, we went up to the roof of the hotel and sunned ourselves. And all those European men were wearing skimpy bathing suits.* Harry smiled at the memory. "That was a lot of eye candy."

Harry reflected as he took another bite of the apple. They'd been young, invincible. Nothing could stop them. Not long before, he'd thought he'd never find anyone to share his life with. Then Richard had come along and taken hold of him.

You were innocent. I couldn't resist.

Harry leaned against the counter as he savored the last of the apple. Beetle was nearby in a sit position, staring up at him. His brown eyes seemed to search Harry's face as if waiting for a word he'd recognize, like *eat, treat,* or *play.*

Innocent, Harry thought. *You certainly brought me out of my shell.*

Hey, I didn't bring you out … I launched you out.

"You were never ashamed," Harry said. *Never wished to be anything but who you were.*

Who else could I be? It's too silly to even imagine.

Harry nodded. *You've always been a mystery to me,* he thought, as he tossed the apple core into the trash. "How did you manage to be so confident?"

It helped that I'm not crazy like you, the voice echoed.

I suppose so, Harry agreed, as he added water to Beetle's bowl. "There you go, boy. How's that?"

Beetle lapped at the bowl, splashing liquid on the floor. Harry grabbed a paper towel and wiped it up.

"Okay … come on, boy. Let's get to work. We can't stand around all day talking if we ever expect to finish that novel."

Beetle looked up, giving Harry his full attention.

"Come on," Harry repeated, and with a wave of his hand, Beetle charged down the hall and disappeared into Harry's office.

2

Rita waited impatiently for the dryer to enter its final spin cycle.

She hated laundry day.

Why an eight-story apartment building with twenty apartments per floor had a laundry room with only four washing machines and four dryers was a maddening mystery. To beat the rush, Rita arrived at six-thirty in the morning, and even at that early hour, one or two loads were already up and running. Even so, she refused, unlike many of her neighbors, to sit on the hard, wooden bench near the door, reading a novel, and waiting to move the laundry from the washing machine to the dryer and then onto the folding table. And now that she drove Rikki to school in the morning, she had to be on the road somewhere between adding the fabric softener and the final rinse. Neighbors left angry notes in her laundry basket, complaining about her inattention to the timing of the chore. Lately, she'd found wet clothes sitting in the white plastic laundry basket atop a commandeered washing machine, waiting to go into the dryer.

"Don't these people have anything better to do?" Rita had complained to Rikki as she prepared dinner. A hot rotisserie chicken from the grocery store sat on the counter, waiting to be carved.

Rikki held the offending note in her hand. "This says you left the laundry sitting for over forty-five minutes."

Rita sniffed. "You know Tuesday is my day off. I get distracted. Regis and Kelly were on."

"Well, that doesn't seem right," Rikki confessed, siding with the neighbors.

Rita snorted as she hacked at the chicken. "It's like living in China or India," she declared, though she'd never been to either place. "People on top of people."

Rikki crushed the note into a ball. "And they're all going through our laundry."

"Oh?" was all Rita could manage, her eyes wide with the sudden realization. "They are!" She held the carving knife in the air. "Examining our dainties. Touching our clean clothes with their grubby hands."

And so Rita made a decision. She would pay closer attention. Perhaps bring a magazine with her.

The next Tuesday, she was there early. *God, it's hot in here,* she thought, as she scanned a *Reader's Digest* and waited for the dryer to go into a final spin. The intense floral smell of detergent permeated the place. *This is Seymour's fault,* she groused as her eye settled on a Holland America Line advertisement to cruise the Caribbean. *We could have had a house,* she raged, still thinking of her former husband, even though they'd divorced decades ago and the poor man was long dead.

A stray voice broke her inner tirade.

"Rita?"

It was Helen Winer from 3L.

In her early forties, Helen was dressed like a teenager in tight blue jeans, sparkly red sneakers, and a high-necked top that hung loosely about her emaciated frame. *Dear God,* Rita thought. *Eat something, for Christ's sake! I'm nauseated just looking at you.* But instead she said, "Oh, Helen. I didn't see you there." Smiling to herself. *You must have slid under the door.*

"I only just came down," Helen answered, laundry basket in her veiny hands as she scanned the room. "Not one machine free? Can you believe this?"

"It's a full house," Rita intoned in her most charming voice. "I'm in dryer number two."

Helen lifted the basket and placed it atop one of the running washers. Turning to Rita, she smiled. "There, now I have a reserved spot."

Rita let out an awkward laugh, all the while wondering if it was Helen who'd been leaving her those nasty notes.

"So how's Rikki doing?" Helen asked, taking a seat next to Rita. "Are you still driving her to school?"

"Oh, she's doing just fine," Rita answered, dismissing the topic with a wave of her hand. "That happened ages ago. You know how kids are. They adjust."

"But that was *horrible,*" Helen continued. "If it had been Barbra, we would have moved. Lenny would have insisted. But then Rikki doesn't have a father? Barbra told me that Rikki's mother never married. Such a shame. A girl should have a father. A man in her life."

Rita took it all in. Helen's attitude, body language, and tone. As she listened, she wondered where anyone got off judging her or her granddaughter. She was doing the best she could. She hadn't expected to be raising a teenager at this time in life. Lord knows it tested the limit of her maternal skills, which had been severely challenged raising her own kids. The plan had been that, after Seymour, she'd remarry. Preferably a rich man. She'd be off somewhere traveling, enjoying the good life, instead of passing her days with the likes of women like Helen.

"Well, if you'll excuse me, I have to get going," Rita said, standing up, desperate to get away as her dryer approached the end of the spin cycle.

"But your wash?" Helen pointed at the dryer. "You haven't taken your clothes out of the dryer yet."

Rita blinked. "Yes, well, I just remembered. I have something in the oven. I better get it out. Then I'll be right back down."

Helen shook her head in disapproval. "It's okay with me as long as I'm not waiting for that dryer."

Rita offered a curt smile. *You can drop dead for all I care,* she thought, as she left the hot room.

◆

"I can't remember her," Rikki said, dish towel in hand, drying a dinner plate.

They stood together at the sink, Rita in a pair of yellow Playtex gloves washing, Rikki drying.

"It's been years, and I still can't remember."

Rita gave Rikki a disapproving glance.

"Talk to me about El," Rikki begged, while Rita squeezed more dishwashing soap onto the sponge. "Please, Rita."

With her bright red hair slicked back, no makeup to cover her blotchy, pale skin, Rita looked every inch of her seventy-four years. Rikki wondered if she, too, might age like Rita. The mere thought gave her the shivers.

"You could never forget your mother," Rita said as she pushed the suds around in the sink, scraping off bits of charred eggplant from the broiler pan. She'd tried to prepare the vegetable without frying. It was a trick shared by a coworker. Unfortunately, she'd failed to remember to spray the pan, and the eggplant stuck.

"But *I can't remember her*," Rikki insisted. "I don't understand. Didn't the doctor say that I'd eventually remember?"

"You were very sick, dear. Remember, you didn't talk for three months."

But Rikki didn't remember. That was the whole point. "Yes, but that was then. I'm talking now."

"But you're well now," Rita said, as she rinsed a dinner glass. "You're in school. Good grades. Why do you want to talk about a time when you were ill?"

"I want to remember," Rikki pressed. "I have to remember."

"She loved you very much," Rita stated, as if by describing Rikki's mother's affection it might fill Rikki's void.

Rikki shook her head. "It's good to hear, but that's not the same as feeling the love yourself."

Rita persisted. "Your mother used to say that nothing in the world would ever be as important to her as you. Nothing." And then she gasped, bringing a soapy glove to her mouth to stifle a cry.

"Oh, Grandma," Rikki said, a sweetness in her voice, as she put down the dishtowel. She rarely referred to Rita as Grandma, but during these moments, Rikki forgot the protocol. "Are you okay?" she asked, rubbing Rita's back. "I didn't mean to upset you."

Rita shook her head and held onto the edge of the sink, leaning forward as the hot water from the tap continued to splash onto soiled silverware. "Forgive me," she blurted out, as she struggled to pull herself together, tears flowing down her cheeks.

"Okay," Rikki sighed, an arm about Rita, comforting the older woman. "We don't have to talk about it. It's okay."

"I can't," Rita said, in an apologetic tone. She gasped for air between sobs. "It's a horrible thing to lose a child … I don't think I'll ever … ever get over it. How could this terrible thing have happened?" She offered Rikki a pitiful look. "I wasn't a perfect mother and I'm certainly not a perfect grandmother, but I didn't deserve this," she continued, shoulders slumped, chin pressed to her chest.

"No, of course not," Rikki said.

When Rita finally looked up, Rikki used her dishtowel to wipe the soapsuds from her grandmother's face.

"I'll never recover. And I just can't think about it." Rita shook her head in defiance. "Such dreadful things shouldn't ever happen."

Rikki didn't know what else to say. It had always been this way. Ever since she came to live with Rita. She couldn't remember her mother, and Rita was unable to talk about El. And because they didn't talk, Rikki feared she might never remember.

It was as if El had never been born.

Rikki removed her grandmother's gloves. "Why don't you go sit down and rest. I'll finish up."

"Are you sure?" Rita asked, eyes still glistening.

Rikki gave Rita's arm a squeeze. "Yes, now go ahead."

◆

Estelle Ida Goldenbaum had always hated her name.

Raised with girls named Susan, Lauren, Hope, and Linda, she couldn't help feeling that the name Estelle was part of a much older generation of women named Fanny, Bertha, Irma, and Gertrude. So when Estelle had turned fifteen, she made a decision. She confronted her parents during dinner, and while her father poked at the broccoli on his plate, Estelle made her announcement. "I'm changing my name to El." She glanced from one parent to the other. "El. E...L. It's short and easy to spell."

Her brother giggled.

Only two years younger, Rick was a slight, scrawny, blonde boy with thick glasses. "That's what they call the elevated train in Chicago!" he cried out in delight, his eyes seeming even smaller in the heavy black frames.

Estelle closed her eyes and tried to ignore her brother.

"I was just reading about it in the library. The first stretch was 3½ miles and opened in June 1892. At first, it was powered by a steam engine, but then in 1893, the third-rail electrical power system was introduced..."

Dear God, she thought. *Why does he have to be so darn smart?*

"...at the 1893 World's Columbian Exposition."

"Rick...we're eating. That's enough," Rita said with irritation.

When Estelle opened her eyes, her brother was looking up at her, a hurt expression plastered on his gentle face. His eyes seemed to be waiting for her response to the information he had offered. Instead, Estelle just shook her head, hoping he'd take the hint and stop talking. He did.

Her father, Seymour, offered a beleaguered look as if the difficulties of life had inflicted upon him a perpetual frown. He glanced over at Estelle's mother. "Rita, what's this all about?" The dark circles under his eyes seemed even more pronounced than usual.

Rita shrugged. She reached for a glass of water and took a sip.

"I'm serious," Estelle whined. "My name is ridiculous. All the kids tease me. They're calling me Essie. I hate it."

"Estelle was my grandmother's name," her father said, focused intently on his daughter. "You don't get to decide your name. That's something that is given to you. Offered in love. Children don't give back their names."

"I don't care what you say. It's my life!" El shrieked as she jerked herself away from the table with such force that her water glass nearly tumbled over. "I'm tired of being Estelle." She stood in defiance. "My name is El."

"Sit back down," Rita said in a firm tone, glaring at her daughter. "Where are your manners?"

Estelle defiantly stood behind her chair as if it were a shield. It all seemed so hopeless. The two adults before her would never understand. How could she ever get them to take her seriously?

"Sit down," Rita again ordered as Estelle slinked back down into her seat.

Her father wiped his mouth with a napkin as he looked over at his daughter.

It seemed to Estelle that he was seeing her for the first time.

But even as he looked at her, he directed his comments to his wife. "Rita, I've had a long day. Can't we have a quiet dinner?" His mouth settled back into its usual frown.

Rita glared across the table at her husband. "I'm sorry if this is all too much for you," she said indignantly. "Seymour, you're not the only one who works in this family. You should see the bunions on some of those women who come into the store. God. You've never seen such feet. And if you think being a mother, making dinner, and cleaning this apartment doesn't entitle me to a little peace and quiet too—well—you're wrong."

Seymour took a breath. "I'm not having an argument. It's already been a long day."

Estelle shifted nervously in her seat. She hadn't realized that her demand would bring on another family fight. All she wanted to do was change her name. Was that too much to ask?

Rita had one elbow on the table as she leaned forward. "I'm tired too, Seymour."

"Tired?" her father snapped, his head slightly tilted to the right. "*You're* tired? You drive fifteen minutes to Bayside to sell ladies' shoes. I take the New York City bus and subway system to Manhattan... pushed and shoved through filth... to work a ten-hour day for an accounting firm that doesn't even know my name." Her father's voice began to escalate. "They tell me I'm not up for a promotion because they want to recruit new talent." He shook his head in disgust. "New talent... when I've given my life to that company."

"Seymour," Rita said, shaking her head, signaling that it was neither the time nor the place for his comments.

'No," Seymour answered. "It's time she learned that she's not the center of the universe. The world doesn't revolve around her little blonde head."

Rita reached for her pack of cigarettes.

"I wish you wouldn't," Seymour said. "It's like kissing an ashtray."

Rita lit up, taking a deep inhalation. She exhaled. "And since when are you interested in kissing?" she said in a dismissive manner.

Seymour pulled the napkin from his lap and tossed it on the table. "Fine," he said, hands in the air. "I give up. You smoke," he told his wife, "and you," looking at his daughter, "can call yourself anything you want. As long as you're both happy," he said getting up from the table, "God knows, I'm not."

◆

Harry stretched his neck. Why had he ever agreed to do a Microsoft *Live Meeting* with his editor?

The screen came to life as Edward Heaton flashed into view. In his mid-forties, Edward had a baby face. He'd often been mistaken for Neil Patrick Harris.

"Hey, Harry, how are you feeling?" Edward asked, a bright smile lighting up the screen.

"I'm fine," Harry winced, adjusting himself in his seat. "My back's a little stiff and I've been getting these terrific headaches."

"Have you gone to the doctor yet?" Edward asked, expressing genuine concern.

"No," Harry demurred. "You know I hate doctors. Almost as much as I hate editors."

"Nice one, Harry," Edward laughed. "After all these years of working together, I thought we were friends."

"That depends," Harry said, stroking the stubble on his chin. "Did you like the first three chapters?"

"Harry, it's just too predictable. You've got to mix it up. The plot is too similar to the last book. No one wants to pay good money to read the same story."

Harry shifted nervously. "Well, I think it's good," he said indignantly, faking an air of confidence. "I think it's my best work yet."

Edward peered into the screen, grimacing, cheeks pulled high, lips pressed tightly together. "Not quite," he said. "Not by a long shot."

"What happened to your glasses?" Harry asked.

Edward arched his brows. "I had laser surgery. I told you about it last week. I just did it yesterday."

Harry nodded. He remembered. "And you're back working so soon?"

"It didn't hurt. It was one-two-three, done," Edward said snapping his fingers.

"That's the problem with the world today," Harry muttered, mostly to himself.

Edward leaned in closer to the screen. His nose, beautifully straight and well-proportioned for his face, became a projectile as if reflected by a fun-house mirror. "What did you say? I can't hear you."

"See," Harry blasted. "You're leaning in, thinking you'll be able to hear me better. You stupid bastard. You can't hear me any better. I'm not there."

"Oh, Harry," Edward reproached him. "Is this about those chapters?"

Harry pounded on his desk with his fist. "*Everything* is about those chapters."

"Now, don't lose your temper," Edward advised. "We've done this before. Just start again. And this time, pull the reader in quicker. You write murder mysteries. That's your genre. That's what sells. And it's like I always say..."

Harry completed the sentence: "...if you write for your readers, you'll have a best-seller. I know."

"Especially when they're eagerly awaiting your next book."

Harry nodded, dejected. "Yes, I mustn't disappoint my audience. I get it."

"Good," Edward said. "I'll check back with you next week. Give Beetle a treat from me."

Harry turned to the terrier curled up in his dog bed, fast asleep. "Beetle just gave you the finger," Harry said, holding his middle finger up to the screen.

"Nice," Edward laughed. "So glad you can take constructive criticism. Why not use all that anger in your writing? It'll make those scenes jump right off the page."

◆

Rikki turned the corner and walked past the Chinese laundry, the dry cleaner, the candy store, and the barbershop. The eight-story building where she lived with Rita came into view. Terraces painted an aqua blue contrasted sharply with the red brick. Aguilar Gardens—an odd name, considering there were no flowers, just a contiguous cement walkway bordered by a chain-link fence and 3×5 *Keep Off the Grass* signs posted every twenty feet to guard a strip of greenery that bordered the building.

A raspy voice called out as Rikki approached the front steps. "Rikki, how's your grandmother feeling?"

Rikki winced.

It was Mrs. Mandelbaum from 6G. Her apartment was right across from the elevator on Rikki's floor. The old woman often popped her head out, surprising Rikki as she waited for the elevator. "That Mrs. M is such a yenta," Rita had warned Rikki. "Be careful about being too friendly. Not everyone needs to know our business."

Despite the chilly weather, Mrs. M had set up a folding chair on the sidewalk, amid the crowd of other seniors. As the old woman sat with her legs crossed, Rikki could see her pink and green housedress, paired with a blue winter peacoat. Her white hair, clipped short in a boyish cut, exposed tiny, bat-like ears. Rikki imagined those ears in a 360-degree rotation as Mrs. M clocked the arrival and departure of everyone on the sixth floor, distinguishing tenants by their footsteps. Twenty steps. The Millers in 6D. Forty steps. The Greens in 6M.

"I haven't seen her since yesterday," the yenta said, as if she was in charge of attendance at Aguilar Gardens. "Is she okay? Do I need to stop by and check on her?"

Rikki tried to keep a poker face. The mere prospect of Mrs. M entering the apartment and snooping around was abhorrent. "Oh, no. She's fine," she reassured the older woman.

Rikki hated living in the high-rise. Except in the dead of winter, seniors congregated at the front of the building to pass the time, mostly gossiping, and, according to Rita, annoying their neighbors. Some brought their own folding chairs, like Mrs. M, while others just milled about, leaning against the handrails, and in warmer weather sitting on the steps, blocking access to the front door. They seemed to know, or appeared entitled to know, everyone else's business.

And they weren't only out front.

They were in the lobby, the laundry room, and on the benches out back by the cement playground. Milling around, asking questions, prying with their eyes. Wondering how Rikki was doing in school, where she was coming from, where she was going. A million questions. Sharp tones, demanding voices, probing Rikki and Rita's personal business out on the street for everyone to hear.

"Rita's fine," she answered, knowing it was a difficult day for her grandmother, but hoping to end the questioning.

The group of adults turned their attention to Rikki. Dull eyes fired, imaginations blossomed, as Rikki sensed judgments being formed. She wanted to stab Mrs. M with her Bic pen, but then the Bic was her favorite and she saw no reason to sacrifice a perfectly good pen for the likes of Mrs. M.

The truth was that Rita had taken to her bed. It happened every year on El's birthday. Rita became inconsolable. And though Rikki, too, felt upset, her reasons were different. She didn't suffer the physical collapse that Rita endured. How could she, when she remembered nothing of her mother? Still, she was certain that she must have loved her mother very much. Hadn't she been hospitalized for three months? Didn't she have to regularly see a psychiatrist? And yet, when Rita fell apart, Rikki found herself distracted. Frightened by the intensity of the older woman's grief.

"Then why haven't I seen her?" Mrs. M continued to push.

Rikki started to make her way past. "I can't really say," she admitted, "but she's absolutely fine."

Mrs. M wasn't quite through. "Are you sure, dear? The flu is going around. How are you feeling? You don't look well."

All eyes again turned on Rikki.

"I feel very well, Mrs. Mandelbaum," she boldly answered, looking from one adult to the other. "Perhaps you shouldn't be sitting out here in the cold. *It is November*. And you're not a young woman," Rikki blurted out as she rushed up the steps, desperate to get away.

"Your grandmother has raised a very rude young lady," Mrs. M. shouted.

"Thank you, Mrs. Mandelbaum," Rikki called back. "I'll be sure to let her know."

◆

Lil struggled to concentrate, even as she reminded her students about the importance of quieting their minds while maintaining the fullness of the breath. It was the end of class. The room was dark. About her, thirty students lay on their backs, eyes closed. She sat cross-legged on the floor before them, her thoughts straying to her handsome neighbor, Harry Aldon.

It's a shame a man like that should be alone. I must invite him to dinner.

She instructed the class to take another deep breath, hold, and release.

I wonder if authors make any money. Oh, it'd be so nice to be with a man of quality. Someone who I could really trust.

She visualized the cover of Harry's latest book, which had been delivered to her front door courtesy of Amazon. The silhouette of a young man stood dangerously close to the edge of a cliff, arms extended, ready to jump. The title was displayed in bold black letters—*Death Leap*—set against a burnt-orange background.

She shifted her hips, releasing tension in her lower buttocks. *What kind of title is that? It's so dark.* She licked her lips and tried to refocus on her breath.

Her last two relationships had proven a disaster. Walter had turned out to be an on-line cheater. She'd found him trolling Internet sites. *He told me that we were exclusively dating,* she remembered with irritation. She'd trapped him by creating a bogus account on Match.com.

And then there was Peter. He'd broken her heart.

Such a lovely man, she'd thought, when they first met. Kind and affectionate, but unable to maintain an erection. *I'm too young to be celibate. I still have my needs,* she thought as Peter sat on the edge of the bed, embarrassed and apologetic. *Such a shame.* A successful lawyer. She'd so hoped Peter would be the one.

And then, the others. So many others.

Looking back, she wondered if she'd been too picky. No, she surmised. She had standards. And yet, it saddened her to think that she'd never married.

Don't focus on the negative, she berated herself. *You have a wonderful life. Not many women who are married can say that.* She suddenly felt superior. *And it's not like I chose to be single.* Though she couldn't help but wonder if her personal energy, strong and decisive, had created her current circumstance.

With a final breath she roused the class, instructing her students to open their eyes and, when ready, to sit up. Slowly, the group came to life, assuming a posture that mirrored her own. She raised her palms to her chest, pressing them together in the guise of prayer and slowly bowed at the waist. In unison, the group said, "*Namaste.*"

◆

Crossing the Aguilar Gardens lobby, Rikki spotted three adults waiting by the two elevators. She considered ducking down the hall, but it was too late. They'd seen her, turned, and smiled. So she marched forward, politely saying hello, per Rita's rules. *Always say hello when you meet people at the elevator. When the elevator doors open, stand back, and allow everyone to exit. If you're by the buttons, ask the others what floor they would like. When you arrive at your floor, say, "Goodbye." And most of all, never fart or belch in an enclosed space. People will talk.*

The two gray-haired women were in the midst of a lively conversation. Something about a sale going on at Macy's. The other woman was younger, a brunette with shoulder-length hair. She wore a black leather jacket over a pair of fitted jeans. Rikki couldn't help but notice her brown high-heeled boots. The four-inch heels were so thin, Rikki wondered how they didn't just break off.

Rikki focused on the lighted displays above each elevator as she peripherally sensed Ms. Boots staring at her. Rikki touched her face, hoping she didn't have a zit popping up. Floors eight, seven, six… the elevators were seemingly tied in a race to the lobby. Then, one elevator stopped on the fifth floor while the other continued on to the fourth floor.

"Are you El's daughter?" the younger woman finally asked.

Three, two, one. Rikki smiled.

"You look so much like her. The hair is different—but your face. It's a mirror image. I can't get over it."

The doors of the elevator opened to the lobby.

"My name is Jenny. Your mother and I went to school together. We ran into each other a few years ago when my mother moved into 5J."

Rikki nodded as all four entered the elevator. Jenny stood next to Rikki at the back. The two older women stood at the front, entering everyone's floor as it was called out and continuing to talk, but their conversation had shifted to the narrow aisles at the supermarket.

"Just last week, this dreadful woman clipped the back of my heel with her cart," Rikki overheard one say to the other. "I think she did it on purpose."

As the elevator doors closed, Rikki was struck by the intense mix of female scents: orange citrus combined with honey violet and a hint of lilac. Rikki cleared her throat, suppressing the urge to sneeze. She spied flakes of dandruff on the dark woolen coat of the woman in front of her. Oddly, it reminded Rikki of coconut. And then the woman sneezed. Rikki gasped, holding her breath as the elevator passed the first floor.

"Whatever you do," Rita had warned her, "don't touch the buttons in the elevator with the tips of your fingers. Use your knuckle. Those elevators are a breeding ground for germs. So toxic, someone should call in the CDC."

Jenny smiled as she looked at Rikki. "I haven't seen your mother in years. How's she doing?"

Rikki jerked her head from side to side as she held her breath, afraid she might be forced to take another breath before getting off the elevator.

The elevator stopped on the fifth floor—Jenny's stop. As she left the car, she turned to Rikki, placing a hand on the rubber bumper that kept the elevator doors from closing. Instead of saying goodbye, as Rikki assumed she would, Jenny said, "I'd love to see her again. Please let her know."

The other two women in the car turned to look at Rikki, who had yet to answer. Rikki finally exhaled, now gasping for breath as she said, "I can't."

"Why not?" asked Jenny, a troubled look on her face.

"Because she's *dead!*" Rikki blurted out, exasperated by having to explain. As soon as the words left her mouth, she felt a deep shame, as if El had somehow abandoned her because she was unlovable.

Jenny's face went pale. "Oh, my God." She stepped back from the elevator, her face registering a pained expression, confirming to Rikki that her personal tragedy was just as awful as she believed it to be.

◆

Harry shielded his eyes from the bright Phoenix sun as he hurried along the walkway past five identical, three-story white buildings in search of building A.

There must be a sign somewhere, he thought, as he crossed a maze of pathways, spying one door and then another. He imagined old people wandering aimlessly, constantly lost in their own housing development. *This is really impossible,* he decided as a woman above called out "Yoo-hoo!" Harry looked up. He spotted a large letter A plastered high on the corner of the building.

"Damn," he said. *I was supposed to look up. Why didn't I look up?*

"Yoo-hoo!" she called again, hand waving from the terrace. It was a sunny eighty-five degrees, and she was dressed in a bright yellow sweater. "Are you my ride?"

Harry smiled. "I'm your guy," he said loudly, just in case she was hard of hearing.

"I'll be right down. Don't go anywhere."

It was Tuesday, the day Harry drove seniors to their doctors' appointments. He'd been doing it for three years, ever since he'd decided that writing full-time had become too isolating. Today, he was picking up Mrs. Adeline Jones.

"You can take someone grocery shopping or drive them to their doctor's office," Sue, the volunteer coordinator from Duet, had informed him at the volunteer orientation session.

Harry hated the idea of going supermarket shopping. Not being much of a cook, he found supermarkets overwhelming. Carts darting in and out of the aisles and those long check-out lines. "I'll take the medical appointments," he answered, worried that he might not be up to the task. Small talk had never been his thing. But fortunately, most of his riders were eager to chat. They often talked from the moment his car left the curb until he dropped them back home. They reminisced about relatives, friends, and the places where they had lived; childhoods, marriages, and children. They provided an oral history of a vanishing generation. The Great Depression. World War II. The McCarthy years. Harry listened intently, mesmerized by their stories, pleasantly distracted from his own concerns.

"Let me get that door," he said as Mrs. Jones approached the passenger side of his Ford Escape. Her posture was perfect. Probably no taller than five feet, the little lady bent forward at the waist, placing a large wicker purse with a mother-of-pearl clutch on the car floor. "Oh my, this is a big car," she said sweetly as she hoisted herself in with a firm pull.

"Watch your head," Harry warned out of habit, though her head was nowhere near the car's roofline.

"Aren't you a nice young man?" Mrs. Jones cooed as Harry settled into the driver's seat. "And so polite."

Harry smiled and nodded. "Ah, thank you. But I'm not young."

"That all depends," Mrs. Jones said. "How old are you?"

"Fifty-five come January."

"Hmm," she hummed. "Well, I'm eighty-five." Her tone was boastful.

"No," Harry said, turning to inspect the lovely lady next to him. "I don't believe it."

"Well, it's true," she said, giving him a sideways glance. The twinkle in her eyes was coy. Almost seductive. He could sense her examining his face even as the car pulled forward.

"You know, when I look at you," she started, "I'm reminded of my third husband, Edgar."

"Third husband?" Harry said, bemused, as the Ford left the parking lot heading west on Camelback.

"Yes," she said, head held high. "You wouldn't know it, but I was once a pretty hot number. I worked as a stewardess in 1946 for United Airlines."

"Oh," Harry said, looking at the still very pretty woman. He imagined her young. It wasn't difficult.

"A lot of people don't know it, but back then, we had something called lap time."

Harry made a right on 32nd Street as he listened.

"Newbies had to sit on the pilot's lap. It was kind of a rite of passage."

"Really?" Harry said. "That doesn't seem appropriate."

"Oh, we didn't mind. It was fun. You know, back in those days, they weighed you every week. And you couldn't hold the job if you were over the age of thirty-two."

Harry was appalled. "That seems so wrong. Didn't that bother you?"

"Oh, no." Mrs. Jones smiled as they pulled into the parking lot of the medical office building. "That's the way it was and I just loved it."

◆

Rikki sat on the bed, an open diary across her lap.

Her room, painted a bright yellow, was anything but cheery. It had once been a den, but with Rikki's arrival, Rita had removed the coffee table and added a single bed, which now faced a canvas sofa. Her desk, a wooden folding table Rita had swiped from the storage room, sat at the head of the bed. The walls, covered in posters of matadors, red capes high in the air poised to face the charge of the bull, had been collected during Rita's many trips to Mexico. Small clay pots sat on shelves above the tan sofa. A tall black warrior sporting a sword and red, white, and blue feathers stood on a side table guarding the only picture of Rikki's mother in the house. A 3 × 5 photograph encased in a silver frame.

Rikki held the frame in her hand as she stared at the picture. The photo was of El's high school graduation, a carefully posed, static moment in cap and gown that seemed to obscure any real sense of El's personality. Rikki had spent hours staring at the photograph. Studying it. Trying to animate the smile. Wondering how her mother might have moved her head when she spoke. Raised her eyebrows as she asked a question. Smiled when she expressed love. And how did her voice sound? Rikki was certain that if she could only hear her mother's voice, the memories would flood back. But now, as she looked at the photograph, she felt frustrated. The face seemed familiar. But was it because it was the last thing she looked at before closing her eyes at night? She just couldn't be sure.

"Great traumas can result in a loss of memory. It's the way the brain protects us," Dr. Gillian, the psychiatrist at Sun Haven, had explained. A grandfatherly man with wispy white hair and a long, prominent nose, Gillian generated a kindness that had captured Rikki's trust at the start. "You mustn't be too hard on yourself. When you're ready, you'll remember. It'll come back in bits and pieces. Slowly. Very slowly."

But that had been so long ago, and still, Rikki struggled.

Maybe if I focus, Rikki thought as she stared at the photo. And though she wanted to once again ask Rita about El, she decided against it. *What was the point?* she thought, running a hand across the picture. It was abundantly clear that Rita couldn't talk about El without becoming upset.

Rikki had only recently begun to keep the diary, a long-ago gift from Dr. Gillian. It was the only thing that had remained as proof of her time in Sun Haven. Rita had made certain of that. "Write, my child," Dr. Gillian had said. "Your ability to remember is wrapped up in your unconscious. Tap that source and it will all become clearer."

"You're absolutely fine," Rita had pronounced upon first seeing her granddaughter in the dayroom at the psychiatric hospital. "There is nothing wrong with you," she had said with such conviction that Rikki was certain she was lying. "You're as sane as anyone here," Rita whispered, nervously looking about the room at the other in-patients.

But Rikki knew everyone there was crazy.

She was able to recall snippets of her life in Michigan. The house where she was raised. The neighbors. Old schoolmates and friends. It was just the specifics about El that seemed to be displaced. As if her mind had selectively deleted any memory of her mother. And even with the little she did remember of her life before, she was afraid it too would eventually slip away, lost to the darkest corners of her mind. That fear was exacerbated by her disappointment at losing touch with friends and neighbors from her old Michigan neighborhood. Rikki had written letter after letter. Sent holiday cards. And yet there had been no response.

"Some people just don't know how to behave," Rita had offered as one explanation. "They never really cared about you. They certainly didn't offer to help when you needed it. No. That was my job. Oh, but advice. Now *that* they had plenty of to spread around. Well, don't you give them another thought," she'd said, waving a hand in the air. "*Elitist snobs.* Every last one of them. You don't need those people in your life. They're not interested in you. They're all surface. Focused on themselves. Besides, you now live in Queens. You can't expect people from Michigan to stay in touch. Everyone has moved on. They have their own lives and you have *yours*. It's absurd to think that you can maintain friendships at such a great distance."

Perhaps they have all forgotten me, Rikki thought. *Perhaps Rita's right.*

◆

When El Goldenbaum had turned seventeen, she left Queens for Michigan and the Cranbook Academy of Art. Her parents, who had waited until her graduation from high school, separated that year, much to El's relief. They had fought continuously through El's junior and senior year of high school, and when the split finally came that June, El was all too happy to get away.

"But why not go to Queens College?" her mother implored, disappointed that El had opted to attend school so far from home.

El didn't bother to look up as she knelt on the floor packing a duffel bag with her clothes, rolling her jeans and blouses so that everything would arrive wrinkle-free. "Because," she explained, exasperated by Rita's petulance, "it's time to move on. I'm becoming an adult." El said this proudly, though deep down, she wasn't quite certain.

"That packing can wait. Come here," Rita commanded, arms outstretched.

"Mom, please," El implored. "I have to get this done."

"Why is it that whenever I ask you to do something you give me a hard time? Is it so much for a mother to ask her daughter to return her affection?"

The last thing El wanted was another scene. Rita had become almost impossible to live with as the day approached for her to leave. "Okay," she finally agreed, doing as her mother asked and standing to allow Rita to wrap her arms about her.

"You know how I feel about you. You're my special girl." Rita pressed El tightly to her. "It's so hard to let go. You'll see. One day, when you have a daughter, you'll discover how difficult it is to see her grow up and leave." Rita tucked a stray tress of El's blonde hair behind her daughter's ear as El started to pull away.

"Really, Mother. You're holding on too tight," El protested.

"Promise me," Rita said firmly, "that you won't do any late-night partying or go walking alone. And no drugs or sex."

El glared back. "Mother!"

"Now promise," Rita said, crossing her arms, her face set in a determined gaze. "I need to hear you say it."

El exhaled. "It's the '70s. Drugs are everywhere," she answered breezily. "I won't make a promise that I may not keep. I have no idea what's out there."

Rita clasped a hand to her mouth, weighing her daughter's words. El turned her back to finish packing. "Okay," Rita acquiesced, her hands now on her hips. "Marijuana. But no heroin or cocaine. Nothing you snort or inject. Promise."

El crossed her fingers. "Sure," she said, doubtful that she'd ever try those drugs but covering her bases just in case.

"And no sex."

El grabbed a sweater and started to roll it. "Are you serious? I'm going to college, not a convent."

Rita took a breath. "The least you could do is lie."

El took her mother's hand and pulled her over to the bed where the two sat down side-by-side. "Really, mother. It's time for me to live my own life. Now that Daddy and you have split," El continued, "you have to get on with your own life. I wouldn't dream of telling you what to do. That would be silly. You go and find yourself and maybe," and El smiled despite Rita's awful frown, "you too will find a new life."

But Rita's expression didn't change. "I'm over men. I won't remarry. I'm going to be alone for the rest of my life."

El resisted Rita's obvious attempt at manipulation. "Now don't be silly. Besides, you still have Rick. He won't be going to college for another two years."

Rita shook her head in defiance. "He's a boy. It's different."

"I know." El hugged her mother tightly. "But it's time for me to leave."

"I suppose," Rita acknowledged as she wiped a tear away with the back of her hand. "We've always been so close. Your brother keeps to himself. He's distant, quiet. I could never crack that shell."

"Don't be so hard on him," El said. "He's just off in his own world. A lot of boys are like that. Be glad he's so darn smart."

Rita huffed. "Mensa. That's too smart for me."

El laughed. "He's gifted."

"A real genius," Rita said sarcastically. "With a personality to match."

El had heard her mother's objections before. And though there was truth to the fact that Rick was difficult to communicate with at times, El had always known that she was the favored child. That awareness made her feel sorry for Rick, altering her view of her little brother. Between bouts of obnoxious know-it-all behavior, Rick often sat quietly, seemingly dejected, as if observing the family from afar. Once, on a trip to the Amish country, they'd actually left him behind at a rest stop.

"Where's your brother?" Rita had asked El with alarm, who was busy reading in *Teen Beat* about David Cassidy, her favorite pop star, before noticing Rick wasn't in the car. They had all laughed nervously, even joked that being with Rick was like being alone.

"A lot of great company he'll be," Rita mourned as she blew her nose into a tissue. "At least if he had friends … he'd seem normal."

El hated it when Rita picked on Rick. "Mother, he can't help being different."

"Different, all right," Rita agreed.

El covered her ears. "Stop it. I don't want to hear another word about Rick. He's unique. Special. And I love him."

ready**to**read**more**?

Made in the USA
Monee, IL
14 February 2021

59388008R00142